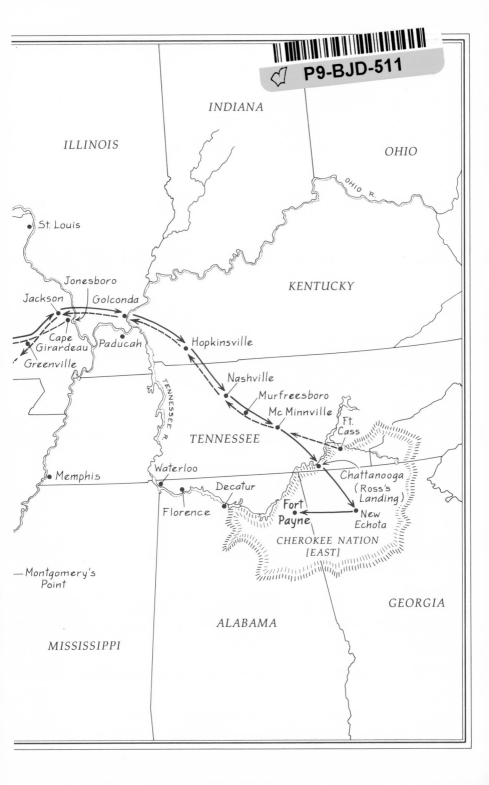

ILLINOIS

INDIANA

OHIO

OHIO R.

KENTUCKY

St. Louis

Jonesboro

Jackson

Golconda

Cape
Girardeau

Paducah

Hopkinsville

Greenville

TENNESSEE R.

Nashville

Murfreesboro

McMinnville

Ft.
Cass

TENNESSEE

Memphis

Waterloo

Decatur

Chattanooga
(Ross's
Landing)

Florence

Fort
Payne

New
Echota

CHEROKEE NATION
[EAST]

Montgomery's
Point

GEORGIA

ALABAMA

MISSISSIPPI

# WALKING
# THE
# TRAIL

# WALKING THE TRAIL

*One Man's Journey Along the*

*Cherokee Trail of Tears*

## BY

# JERRY ELLIS

*Delacorte Press*

Published by
Delacorte Press
Bantam Doubleday Dell Publishing Group, Inc.
666 Fifth Avenue
New York, New York 10103

Manufactured in the United States of America
Published simultaneously in Canada

0-385-30448-X

*For my mother and father*
*and my ancestors in the other world*

# ACKNOWLEDGMENTS

First and foremost, thanks to all the fine folks I met as I walked the Trail of Tears. Without them and the songs of the birds, I might not have made it. Thanks to Dan Potter for all he taught me about the connection between words and the human heart. Brenda Howard for staying strong after she could no longer walk. Emily Reichert, my editor, for her great commitment and sensitivity to the book. Susan Ginsburg, my agent, for being so sharp and supportive. Al Zuckerman, head of Writers House, for introducing me to Susan. Nita Ellis Shoaf for making me laugh at myself, and Sandra Ellis Lafferty for making me reach higher. John Bensink for his encouragement, and Richard L. Stack for being like a brother. Susan Malone and Debbie Maynard for the camping equipment. Beth Kubly for the shelter, and Tyrone Foreman for the book on trees. And you, dear reader, for allowing me into your life for a while.

# FOREWORD

The largest American Indian tribe is the Cherokee, with the 1980 census claiming 232,080 members. By 1800 the Cherokee had intermarried with the Scots-Irish and the British. All it took was a drop or two of Cherokee blood to be considered Cherokee. Some say that Cherokee is not a matter of blood at all, but *a thing of the spirit.*

# AUTHOR'S NOTE

This book is based on my true-life experiences walking the Trail of Tears, although the names and other details of certain individuals have been changed.

# WALKING THE TRAIL

# CHAPTER ONE

I'M SOAKED TO the bone as I walk through a storm down a country road in western Arkansas. I don't mind the wind and rain so much, but I'm scared to death of lightning. If a bridge or barn were in sight, I'd run for shelter. But forget it. There's just me and trees, swaying in the wind. For the first time in my life, I imagine how a mouse might feel the moment he looks up to see a hawk shoot from the sky to drive claws into his tiny heart.

I wear a hat; a black crow feather sticks from it, while a rattlesnake rattler with eight buttons rides snug under the band at the back of my head. Jeans cover my aching legs.

Lightning flashes yellow once again, as if to see if I'll try to run under a rock. I'm tempted.

The road is flooded and small waterfalls shoot from the rock banks. My feet are blistered and on my back is a red and blue backpack weighing fifty pounds. I've walked one hundred miles in six days and I have eight hundred more miles and seven states to go. I promised myself I'd walk the whole way. But have I lied?

I'm forty-one now, but when I was four years old my house was struck by lightning. I was home with my mother and two sisters and we smelled smoke coming from the attic. I was sure the house would disappear in flames and we'd have nowhere to live. My father, a carpenter, came home from work minutes later. He climbed into the attic with a bucket of water and threw it onto the fire. That put out the flames, but he slipped and fell through the ceiling. He crashed atop a piano and onto the floor. I learned then and there that lightning, as beautiful as it is, doesn't give a damn about man.

I walk facing traffic and a truck, hauling horses, roars toward me. The driver leans forward and squints in disbelief. A cigarette dangles from his mouth and he becomes a blur behind windshield wipers.

As the truck shoots past me I'm hit with a blast of wind and water; for a split second I can't see. My hand flies to my hat to grab it just as it jumps from my head. The snake rattler shakes and the smell of horses pierces my wet nose.

The lightning is much closer now, and I recall hiding behind a big chair in the corner of my house during a thunderstorm when I was in the fourth grade. A bolt of fire might get me, I reasoned, but it would have to find me first.

*Boom!* The thunder follows and a car stops. It's a station wagon with the front fender falling apart with rust. The back is loaded with lumber, plastic pipes, and a garden hose coiled like the snake from whom I got the rattler.

The driver motions for me to hop inside, but I hesitate. A

little girl with a candy bar—there's chocolate on her chin—is propped against his shoulder. A Band-Aid is stretched across her temple. The driver rolls down his window.

Get in, he shouts.

The little girl smiles and it's so cozy and dry inside. Water runs down my nose.

I can't, I say. I'm walking the Trail of Tears.

In 1838, the Cherokee Nation thrived in Alabama, Tennessee, Georgia, and North Carolina. The eighteen thousand Indians had their own newspaper, *The Cherokee Phoenix,* published in both English and Cherokee. They raised corn, cotton, hogs, and cattle. They lived in log houses and had long ago put away their scalping knives. They hoped to live in peace where their ancestors had lived for over five hundred years.

But in 1838, President Martin Van Buren, pressured by Georgia, ordered seven thousand soldiers to round up the Indians at gunpoint. Their homes burned before their eyes, while soldiers dug into the family graves in search of gold and silver.

The Indians were thrown into thirteen forts newly built to act as concentration camps. I was born and raised in Fort Payne (Willstown), Alabama, between Lookout and Sand mountains, which was the site of one of those thirteen camps. All that remains of the fort today is its chimney, crumbling among oaks behind a burger joint and a tire company.

The eighteen thousand Indians were forced to march from their homes in Alabama, Tennessee, Georgia, and North Carolina to Oklahoma, then Indian Territory, in the heart of winter. Many had to walk, and their shoeless feet left tracks of blood on the earth and in the snow. Four thousand Cherokee, mostly children and old people, died along that route which has become known as the Trail of Tears.

You can't walk in this rain, says the driver. Swim, maybe.
I'll be okay, I say.
I hope you make it, he says.
He rolls up his window and the little girl waves good-bye with the hand holding the candy. They disappear into the storm and, I walk on. I feel alone, naked with lightning. Where is my faith? Indeed, where is the strength and courage of my ancestors?

# CHAPTER TWO

TWO WEEKS EARLIER.

It's August and I dig a hole in the earth near my cabin atop a hill in north Alabama. I'm surrounded by oaks, hickories, and pines. Crows squawk in the distance and a hawk circles the next hill.

I line the hole, a foot deep and two feet wide, with rocks as big as my head. This will become the center of the sweatlodge to hold the fire when I return from walking the Trail of Tears. I build a dome frame from small hickory poles around the hole in the ground. I wire them together at the top and cover the frame with an old army tent.

Every Cherokee family had a sweatlodge a few yards from its log house. When the winter was unusually severe and cold wind whistled through the cracks of the house, a family could gather in the small sweatlodge and cover itself with bear or buffalo skins to stay warm. It was also used as a place to seek a vision from the Spirit World after undergoing a fast.

The sweatlodge will be a place for me to purge myself when I return from the walk. It's more than that, though. It is a humble temple and prayer to the Earth that I might have a safe journey.

Just what is my plan for this journey? Well, it seems simple enough: I'll walk the Trail to honor the Indians who suffered and died there in 1838. I hope *my* walk will help ensure that others will learn of what happened to the Cherokee and that it will not be forgotten as the years pass. Rather than follow the original Trail from Alabama to Oklahoma, I'll walk from Oklahoma to Alabama as if I were freed to return to my roots, a luxury taken from the Cherokee. I'll chew the fat with folks, with or without Indian blood, along the Trail—which is mostly state and county roads now—and see just what's really going on with Americans today.

It will also be a physical and mental test for me: Can I walk nine hundred miles without falling apart? What adventures await me? What challenges will I face?

But more than that, the walk will be a spiritual journey for me. I long to know more about the man I am, where I came from, and where I am going. I get my Cherokee blood from my father. Both his mother and father were of Cherokee descent. Their blood runs through my veins, but is their spirit in my soul as well? Where is my place in this world, a world so different from that of my ancestors?

I finish building the sweatlodge as the sun sinks on Sand Mountain. Its steep rock cliffs fade into twilight. Indians once lived there in its caves and overhangs. I have found their stone tools, and they have charged the mystery within me as they connect me with time eternal. Laugh at me for believing such things if you must, but it helps me deal with matters I have not yet revealed.

I sit in a swing between two oaks only a few yards from my cabin, admiring the sweatlodge in the moonlight. There's a sense of peace that comes from working with my hands, and I need all that I can find right now. It's only two days before I leave home for the walk, and for the past week I've felt a mixture of excitement and fear.

I'm not so much afraid of some lunatic placing a gun to my head to blow out my brains as I am of being cornered by someone and forced to kill him to save my life. I have no money for a lawyer and I'm not so sure that justice comes without it. I'm horrified at the thought of prison.

But as I swing back and forth between the two oaks in the moonlight, I tell myself that no harm will come to me. What I'm about to do has meaning and purpose. There is a God, or Great Spirit, I tell myself. He will protect me. I sometimes wonder if I flatter myself.

A whippoorwill calls from the darkness and I'm reminded of how lonely I've become the past few months. It's been almost a year since I've slept with anyone and I'm hungry for love. Starved for sex.

The whippoorwill calls again and I consider placing a candle in the cabin window. The Cherokee did this in hopes of drawing the bird closer. They believed it brought the listener sweet dreams.


I was small as a child and had little love for the school bully. It still warms my heart today to remember the moment I knocked the shit out of him after lifting weights for three months.

I was fourteen when that happened and I've been a bodybuilder and weight lifter ever since. In fact, it's iron that has always helped put my life back together after a broken romance or some other emotional whiplash.

While I've been working out harder than usual to prepare for the walk, it isn't my body that concerns me as much as my mind and heart. To the point: I worry that my mother or father may die while I am away. They live at the bottom of the hill from my cabin and I stay with them most of the time. They're my best friends.

Do you have to sleep in a tent? says my mother.

I'll get a motel from time to time, I say.

Nothing wrong with a tent, says my father. Save yourself the money.

Maybe he should sell the tent, says my mother. He could sleep on the ground and cover himself with leaves at night.

No, no, don't be stupid, says my father. Pine needles are softer.

Perhaps I'm just a damned sentimental fool, but I enter my cabin to say good-bye. It's three stories tall and built from pine poles and barn lumber. It began as a treehouse in three towering pines and a large hickory. But the following year I added the first floor to support it from the ground. Part of the fireplace is built from rocks from a chimney my grandfather had made. Even from his grave the old man whispers into my ear. When he moved to Alabama from Virginia he walked almost four hundred miles to get here.

To the right of the fireplace, on the hearth, is a millstone and pestle I found alongside a nearby creek. The Indians used them to grind corn and acorns. Five feet from these stones sits a case filled with arrowheads, celts, and stone knife blades I've found since I was seven years old. Some of them are over ten thousand years old and it isn't easy to accept that I will become dust just like those who made them.

From the third floor I see the glow of lights over Fort Payne. It's an Appalachian community of sock mills and farms. Also, there are a couple of steel mills and the Earth Grain Bakery. Bootleggers and Bible salesmen buy gasoline at the same Stop and Go.

The town's drive-in theater was knocked down for progress a few years back—about the same time Rexall Drugs vanished, along with its soda fountain.

Downtown has, of course, pretty well dried up, compared to the shopping centers where Wal-Mart and K mart aim to please. Twin Cinema offers four whole movies to pick from and McDonald's and Burger King promise to do you right.

We even got cable TV halfway up the mountains. Yes, sir, it's a wonderful Age. Every Southern town is starting to look just like the next one. Best of all, the heart surgery is painless, so they say.

The cabin and sweatlodge disappear into the darkness as I walk down the hill to my parents' house. I load my backpack with clothes, tent, sleeping bag, camera, tape recorder, cooking gear, and a canteen. The canteen is special not only because it's borrowed from my friend, Susan, but because of her history: When the U.S. soldiers forced the Indians on their death march from here to Oklahoma, a Cherokee mother hid her new baby daughter with a white family because she was afraid she would die on the Trail. That baby girl was Susan's distant grandmother.

I lean my pack against the wall and go to bed. I can't sleep because I'm too excited about leaving tomorrow. An owl hoots from a pine just beyond my window. I pray that he will let me into his world as I camp among the trees at night.

Who? He calls. Who?

A friend, I whisper. A friend.

I awake in the night with a train rolling down the tracks a mile away. A dog howls in the darkness.

The August night is usually cool as air drifts down from Lookout and Sand mountains, but tonight is hot and humid. I pull the cover from my naked body and slip into my jeans. I put on my shoes.

I go outside and walk to the garden. I dig my hand into the soil and raise the earth to my nose. I swear I'll remember the smell till I get back home. It's not just dirt; it's my parents and myself. My father and I planted the rows, lush with green beans, squash, corn, tomatoes, okra, turnip greens, potatoes, and more. My mother picks, washes, cans, and freezes them. Our eyes sing to each other about the garden in ways that perhaps only we can understand. We're proud of our conspiracy against processed foods and cloned cans.

You're leaving on this walk at the wrong time, says my father. Corn's just now coming in. Tomatoes'll be ripe by next week.

I walk on through the garden to where a pole with fifteen gourds stands. They have holes for purple martins to build nests, but only blackbirds have done so.

Only a few feet to the right of the gourds, in the corn, is where I killed the rattlesnake whose buttons ride under the band of my hat. I took no pride in blowing it apart with a shotgun, but it was coiled to strike when my mother gathered green beans only a few feet away. She might've gotten a taste of his poison, if our German shepherd, Buddy, hadn't barked to warn her.

I want to die like that German shepherd. He followed my father to the raspberry bushes and curled up in a pile of leaves in sunlight while Daddy filled his bucket. He never woke.

My father buried him in the pasture beside my sister's horse. I'm glad I wasn't here. It hurts to see him cry.

Why don't you get another dog? I say.

No, he says. I'll stop on a perfect death.

The pumpkin vines grow at the other end of the garden and I must walk carefully past the pepper plants and potatoes to reach them. The Cherokee used to say, never step over the pumpkin vines or count the fruit on them, for that could make them fall off. But there's been too much rain this summer and the vines don't look so hot. I'm not so hopeful about pumpkin pie when I return from the Trail in November.

I become excited when I spot a light across the road where my cousin, Gary, lives. He's several years older than me and as a child I always looked up to him. He has the classic Cherokee features of jet-black hair, high cheek bones and dark eyes. Six months ago he disappeared. I hope the light in his house means that he has returned.

His mother and my father were twins. She once carried a rifle back into the woods where her garden grew. She raised the gun to her chest and pulled the trigger. Deciding she had made a mistake, she walked back to her house and was taken to the hospital. She recovered from the gunshot, but died of cancer three years later.

The rifle she used belonged to Gary and to this day I cannot look into his eyes without thinking about his mother, my aunt. He was never the same after she died.

The light across the road turns out to be only moonlight on a window. I hope I don't disappear like my cousin, unless it's into another world where there is less pain and more laughter.

I walk back across the garden and down through the yard into the house. I slip from my jeans and crawl into bed. I wonder who the hell the guy is deep inside me who swore to walk nine hundred miles.

Well, I say. You've gone and got me out on a limb this time.

Yeah, he says. That was the plan.

# CHAPTER THREE

I F LIGHTNING AND thunder are two people having sex, this storm is a form of rape. There's so much rain beating down that the ditches along the road have flooded and water rushes across the asphalt to meet itself, creating a stream in the middle of the road. Water splashes as I walk and my Reeboks have become lead mops. My shoulders and back ache with the fifty-pound backpack, and I haven't eaten since yesterday.

Every curve in the road brings the new hope that a barn will appear where I can seek shelter. Sit under a basswood tree, the Cherokee saying goes. It is never struck by lightning. But as I round the bend I find only more trees—no basswoods—pastures and more *lightning*.

I almost jump when I spot a big black dog on the side of the road with his mouth open to reveal long sharp teeth. But he's dead and starting to swell. His red tongue hangs out and the water tries to float him. I'd like to kick the son-of-a-bitch who ran over him in the ass. But in the next breath I realize I'm just heated from the storm. The guy who hit him may still have a knot in his gut from the moment of impact. For all I know he circled back to bury the mutt and couldn't take it when he saw his face.

I promise not to look into the eyes of the dog as I walk around him. But I look anyway. The long top tooth on the right is chipped.

When I round the next bend, I stop to take the pack from my back. God, does it feel good to be free of the load. If only I were out of this storm and in the dry, I would ask for nothing. Lament no memory. Cling to no dream. Life would be complete.

Lightning strikes so close this time that I swear it's hit a tree only a rock's throw away. My heart pounds and I want to run.

But some foolish pride makes me lift the pack and strap it once again to my back. I'm pulling the lower belt tight around my waist when another *flash* then *boom* shakes the earth itself.

A red pickup with a dent on the front fender stops. The driver's in his sixties and wears a cowboy hat. He rolls down his window.

Having fun? he says.

I tell him why I'm out here.

I'm going about twenty miles, he says. Hop in and I'll give you a lift. Give you a chance to dry some.

I got to walk the whole way, I say.

Hell, boy, he continues. Ain't nobody gonna know the difference.

I will, I say.

He's chewing on a cigar and spits some tobacco out the window. I can't decide if he's pissed because I won't do what he commands, or if he's simply concerned.

You fixed for money? he says.

Yeah, I say. I'm okay. How far to a café or store?

Five, six miles, he says. Just a store. But I wouldn't stop there.

Wind blows rain through his window and onto his face. He squints and works the cigar to the other side of his mouth.

Why not? I say.

Well, he continues, I don't want to scare you none, but people up there just look for trouble. Low-down trouble, if you see what I mean. Hell, I got a little Indian blood myself. You watch where you walk now.

He pulls back onto the road and I almost call out for him to wait, that I've changed my mind. But a moment more he's gone, and I walk on to discover his cigar floating in the ditch. Funny, how quick you can feel close to someone in a storm and not even know his name.

I wish a woman would stop now and invite me into her car. I wish she would be smooth and warm and believe in things of the heart. I wish I could hold her and forget that I'm just a speck in the rain.

I lower my head so my hat will protect my face from the wind and water. I walk on.

# CHAPTER FOUR

THE DAY I'M to leave Alabama, I awake charged with excitement as if my brain releases some rare chemical stirred by the right challenge. The sun is golden on the morning dew and a mockingbird sings atop the walnut tree just beyond my bedroom window. Like all birds, he is sacred to me now, but when I was a kid I notched my BB gun each time I killed one. Even when a shot didn't kill but hit a bird, it was magic to watch feathers fly and drift against a blue sky. I'm not sure of the day I made a connection between my mother's eyes and those of a bird, but it was the same day magic began to make me feel things I'd never felt before. I sure didn't have the slightest understanding of just how strong a boy had to become to protect that gentleness within.

The mockingbird flies from the top of the walnut tree down

to a pine stump as I put on my jeans. Fresh air drifts through the window and I feel like I'm eighteen instead of forty-one.

A knock at my door.

You up? says my mother.

I know her tone as well as I know her face. She's trying to sound cheerful to hide her fear. Her head is filled with sensationalism from TV talk shows. She's afraid I'll be killed or simply vanish from the face of the earth.

I've decided not to go, I say.

*What?* she says.

Just checking your reflexes, I say.

I tie my shoe strings and look out the window once more. The mockingbird has left the pine stump, but I hear his sweet song somewhere among the trees. I hope some kid doesn't notch his gun while I'm gone.

Good biscuits, I say at breakfast.

You'll phone from time to time? says my mother.

Hell, says my father. It's not like he's going off to war.

It's a hobby of mine to study how my father deals with his emotions when he's worried. Besides saying stuff like he just did, he sucks saliva through two front teeth and has just about mastered the art of keeping his lips together. The sound it creates, like that of a straw at the bottom of a great malt, is another matter.

Don't worry, I say. I'll phone every week or two.

My father opens the trunk of his car and I place my red and blue backpack inside. When he closes it, our cat, Rosco, looms from under the car to rub against my leg as if he senses that I'm leaving. I pick him up and let him be a baby for a moment. Upside down, he ponders the sky and treetops as if just now remembering that they're up there.

It's a forty-five minute drive from my house to the Greyhound bus station in Chattanooga, Tennessee, where I'll get a ride to Oklahoma City and then go on to Tahlequah, Oklahoma, the capital of the Cherokee Nation; there I will begin the walk. On the way, a mile from home, we pass Fort Payne's reservoir, blue and silver in sunlight. The lake is fed by an ancient stream called Will's Creek, and when it was built three years ago I searched the dozed and graded earth for relics.

I was startled to find the remains of a grave, scattered over the moist soil. A stone-polished celt lay three feet from an arrowhead and between them was a human leg bone. I got goosebumps when I gathered them in my hands and what I experienced that night, when I ponder it, can still make me sweat and shake as my heart pounds. It's a story that must be told, but I'll wait till the Trail.

# CHAPTER FIVE

I'M ON A Greyhound just a few miles east of Oklahoma City, where tumbleweeds roll into oil wells and billboards brag of the biggest steaks in America. It's so flat that I feel like I can see almost all the way to the Rockies in Colorado.

The first time I came to Oklahoma City was in 1969, when a friend and I were returning from California to Alabama. I was introduced to his cousin, Carole, and I fell hook, line, and sinker in love. It was my last year at the University of Alabama, and I'd hitchhike fifteen hundred miles from Friday afternoon to Sunday night just to spend one night with this redhead. I rode this rocket for six months and hitchhiked back and forth like this five or six times. People who gave me rides were sometimes curious about my romance.

Were you born crazy, said one man, or did something happen along the way?

She's special. I laughed.

You got a good laugh, he said. Ever thought about recording it? You know, just in case you lose it?

Carole and I were married when I graduated from college. But two years later we were divorced when the distance between our hearts became greater than fifteen hundred miles.

The Greyhound arrives at the bus station in Oklahoma City and I place my backpack in a locker. I'm to spend the night with my friend, Dan, and I can phone him to come and get me, but I'm tired of riding; I'd rather walk to his place, which is about two miles away.

The oil business has been hard on Oklahoma City the past few years, and the neighborhood where Carole once lived now looks like a bomb hit it. Doors and windows are boarded up and broken beer bottles line the street. Carole's apartment was on the ground floor, and I go to the window of the bedroom where we once made love all night. I find a crack in a board and peek inside: The room has no furniture, and blue wallpaper dangles. What the hell, I'd do it all again.

Up the street an Indian with shoulder-length black hair stands on a ladder to paint trim around a window. He eyes the feather sticking from my hat.

How's it going? I say.

Okay, he says. Kind've hot. That a crow feather?

Yeah, I say. It's from my grandfather's land. Back in Alabama.

Crows are mean, he says. But I like 'em.

A fat woman in red pants runs from the house.

You're not a very fast painter, says the woman. What are *you*, a supervisor?

No, I say. I'm just—

I don't need a supervisor, she says.

I walk on as the Indian dips his brush into his bucket. At the corner, I turn to see the woman go back into the house. I reach into my pocket and remove a crow caller my grandfather gave me when I was a child. I bring it to my lips and blow to create the squawk of an excited crow. The Indian turns to me and then to the door where the woman disappeared. With his free hand he makes the motion of a bird in flight, headed for the treetops. I warm inside from the human contact and squawk once more as I head on up the street to the apartment where Dan lives. I knock on his door and it opens.

You're a sight for sore eyes, he says.

I wouldn't trade my two sisters for all the money on Wall Street, but I've always wanted a brother, and Dan is the closest thing to him. He's fifty-seven and a writer who graduated from Yale. The son of an Oklahoma mule trader, he was a recognized novelist and playwright in the sixties, but he let drugs and alcohol take him on a fast train to hell. The past several years, after joining a treatment program, he has stayed clean and is putting his life back together. I'm sad to see his hand shake from time to time like that of someone who has seen something so frightening that the mind deals with the pain by burying it in the flesh itself.

I'm hungry, I say. You up for Denny's?

I can fix us something here, he says, trying to calm his shaking hand.

No, I say. Let's celebrate seeing each other and go out to eat.

At Denny's, Dan and I order the $1.95 breakfast special. I'm happy to see that, at least for the moment, his hand has stopped shaking.

I don't care for the rattlesnake buttons, he says. But the crow feather is a curious touch. Did I tell you my bird story about the poet, e. e. cummings?

You knew him? I say.

When I graduated from Yale, says Dan, I was a caretaker one summer for a wealthy lady in New Hampshire. Her neighbor drove the most beautiful antique car I'd ever seen. I wrote him a postcard, saying how much I admired it. He wrote back and invited me to lunch. The neighbor was e. e. cummings.

Where does the bird story come in? I ask.

Mr. cummings and I became friends, says Dan. His wife took the photograph that's on the back of my first novel. Anyway, he phoned one afternoon to say I should hurry over because something very rare was about to happen. Mr. cummings led us into the living room and said they would be here shortly. We should simply keep our eyes on the window. We waited for what seemed like a long time, but finally, four or five hummingbirds appeared before the window in mid-flight. They nodded two or three times and vanished in the direction of South America.

You pulling my leg? I say.

No, he says. They'd been feeding the birds every summer for several years and had learned their habits. When e. e. died, I drove his wife to the funeral.


That night I stretch out on the couch in the dark to sleep. The window is open and from time to time the Oklahoma wind makes the curtain dance like a ghost. I hear Dan breathing as he sleeps in the next room. When we first became friends, twenty years ago, he told me his greatest fear was to find himself alone as an old man surviving in a hotel room. His small inheritance will be gone in a few months and he's having trouble selling his last two novels. When I close my eyes, I see his hand shaking in the dark. *Oh, my brother, have I told you I love you?*

# CHAPTER SIX

THE NEXT MORNING Dan drives me to the bus station. I catch a Greyhound to Muskogee, Oklahoma. There is no bus service to Tahlequah, capital of the Cherokee Nation, where I will begin walking the Trail of Tears. I'll have to thumb a ride there.

The bus driver pulls my pack from the belly of the bus. I strap it to my back and walk to the outskirts of town. This is the first time I've worn the backpack and I suddenly have a new appreciation of camels. It's almost one hundred degrees and sweat pours down my face and body; my shirt becomes wet.

It's thirty miles to Tahlequah and I raise my thumb to the traffic. The sun shines down in my eyes, but I remove my dark shades so drivers can get a look at the stranger. They pass me as if I'm a sign saying SPEED UP.

*   *   *

By the age of twenty-six I had thumbed enough miles to circle the globe four times. I once rode across the South with the Hell's Angels and camped with Greek Gypsies in Mexico. This thumbing fever began when I was fourteen: I didn't like to wait on the school bus and discovered that I could beat it simply by raising a thumb to the world. It was a major breakthrough because I could meet strangers and get a real education while other students, on the bus, endured the same old routine day in and day out. When I was seventeen I thumbed to New York to visit my sister, Sandra. Picture a boy from the sticks of Alabama gawking at the Empire State Building. Note, however, the realization in his eyes that life back in the South would never be the same again. A new confidence was born.


Come on, I say to the passing cars. I'm not out here to test a new suntan lotion.

An hour passes and I wonder if my luck-of-thumb has gone down the drain. Perhaps now that I'm over forty people feel that I'm too old to bum a ride. Maybe they think anybody who isn't driving his own car has missed the American dream and is just looking for trouble. Maybe their heads are just so rattled by the six o'clock news that, poor souls, they're just plain old afraid of anything or anybody who doesn't fit nice and tight in the peg's hole.

I take off my hat and wipe the sweat from my forehead to remind the drivers that the road isn't air-conditioned. A lot of good this does. Now motorists and passengers are gawking as if I'm a fool who doesn't have enough sense to wear a hat in the sun.

Finally, a truck stops. I lift my pack and run to the door. A man of fifty with scarred hands and Indian eyes studies me.

How far you going? I say, wanting to hear his voice before I hop in.

Tahlequah, he says. If that'll help you any.

I like his voice and I can see deeper into his eyes now.

It sure will help, I say. More than you realize.

I open the door and get in. The man's name is Dub. He lives fifteen miles east of Tahlequah and makes this trip to Muskogee and back every day to pick up and deliver mail. He also raises cattle.

I don't know what it is exactly, he says. But I like to get off by myself sometimes. Just me and the cows out in the pasture. It's not that I don't like people, I do. But animals, well, there's just something special about them.

Yeah, I say. I never met a one yet that carried a gun or robbed.

You worried about dogs on your walk?

Thought I might carry a big stick, I say.

I'd watch out for ticks too, he adds. Little devils carry diseases. The kind that can kill you. I tell you what, he continues. You got to walk right past my house on the Trail. Why don't you stop and spend the night with me and my family?

I got a tent.

You can pitch it there on my farm, he says. Or, we got an extra bedroom. Just make yourself at home. The door's always unlocked, and if I'm not there just walk right in. Help yourself to the food.

This man is almost too good to be true. But my gut tells me that he's as honest as he seems. I'm amazed that the violence and mistrust of today's world hasn't poisoned his mind. He is the perfect medicine to help heal my own suspicion of strangers. Is our meeting no more than coincidence, or is my simple prayer being answered in which I ask to meet those who will help guide and protect me on the journey? In any event, I arrive in Tahlequah in great spirits.

Thanks for the lift, I say. I'll be taking you up on a place to stay.

# CHAPTER SEVEN

H E DRIVES AWAY and I find myself in the center of town, across the street from the old courthouse, surrounded by trees. It gives me chills to think that this is where thousands of Cherokees planted themselves after being uprooted from their homes back in the mountains where I was born and raised. More chilling yet is to recall the four thousand Indians, mostly children and the elderly, who died along the Trail, to be buried in shallow unmarked graves. It also strikes me that I may very well sleep on those unmarked graves as I walk back home.

I'm ready to get somewhere that's cool, and it's been hours since I ate. I cross the street for a café where two Indians exit. Once inside, the sweat stops pouring and a glass of ice water hits the spot. I order a couple of fish sandwiches and some fries.

Tahlequah (population fifteen thousand), means *two is*

*enough* in Cherokee. When the Indians arrived from the South they had planned to have three chiefs, but one was late. The two who had made it decided that they were the right number and the word stuck.

It slowly sinks in that I'm now on the Trail and on my own. The comforts of home are gone, as is the possibility of seeing friends. Nine hundred miles stretch between me and the end of the journey. Oh, yeah, there were those who swore they wanted to come with me, but they were only dreaming. That's okay. I believe in fate. I'm traveling alone because that's the way it's meant to be. Then, too, this way I can stop and go when I please. I can stick my feet in a cool stream at the drop of my hat or howl at the moon as I stand naked in its wondrous light. There's no power like feeling free.

My food arrives and I'm mighty pleased at the size of the fish sandwiches and the fries. Yes, sir, things couldn't be going better. That is, until I'm taking the top off the ketchup bottle and spot the redheaded girl in the booth across from me. She looks to be about four years old and stands in the seat. Her head is twisted toward me and her eyes are squinted as they drill into me. This isn't a big deal, but her hand makes me uneasy. Her finger points straight at me as if she sees something I don't.

Oh, well, I tell myself, she's just playing a game. When her mother discovers what she's doing, she pulls her down into the seat.

No, whispers the mother.

The little girl and her mother leave the café and I return to the great American art form of slapping a bottle of ketchup on its bottom. Come on, damn it.

Having trouble with the ketchup? says the waitress.

No, no, I say. Just exercising a little before I eat.

In town for the holiday? she says.

Today is Thursday and the Cherokee National Holiday begins tomorrow and runs through Sunday. The dancing and bow-shooting events intrigue me. But it's one-on-one human contact I seek. I want to hear secrets and see emotions. I'm tired of masks, especially my own.

With my thirst quenched and my stomach filled, I grab my pack and leave the café, which has now closed. I follow the waitress's directions seven blocks to the Smith Motel.

I enter the office to the smell of curry. A beautiful East Indian woman greets me with a baby in her arms. A man who I assume is her husband peeks from the adjoining room. He wears a sour expression as if he doesn't approve of how I smile at the woman.

Hi, I say to the man. How are you?

The man's head disappears into the room like a snake into a hole. So much for building bridges. Maybe I should've started with an easier question.

I fill out the registration card and when I get to the category MAKE OF CAR, I write *1989 Backpack Convertible.* When the woman reads it, she looks out the window and finally gets it. I pay her and she gives me the key.

I unlock the door to my room and it smells like someone may have died here. But the bed is firm and clean and there's a color TV to distract my nose.

I hop into the shower and wash away the day's sweat. It may not turn me into a new man, but it makes me feel better about the one inside my skin.

Night is falling as I leave the motel room to explore Tahlequah. Downtown is only five or six blocks long and all the stores are closed. I wish I knew someone here and pretend to admire furniture in store windows as an occasional car passes. Yes, yes, a

really great hobby, this chair and couch watching; stop and see
for yourself. Why, glory be, there's a new lamp.

The trees around the old courthouse do, however, offer a lift.
I sit on a wooden bench and savor the limbs, wild in the wind.
Their shadows crisscross as a leaf twirls down into my lap. Dust
peppers my face and thunder echoes in the great distance.

I spot a sign up the street that says YE OLD PUB. As I get closer
it's apparent I can forget the red carpet. There are no windows
and rooms for rent are upstairs. I expect a couple of drunk cock-
roaches to stagger from cracks in the wall. I walk into Ye Old Pub
and order a beer.

Miller, I say. Miller Lite.

You drink that brand 'cause you like it, asks a man next to
me at the bar, or have you been suckered in by those slick TV
ads?

I guess a little of both, I say. What do you drink?

Whiskey, he says. Don't matter what kind, long as it does
the trick.

You Cherokee? I ask.

I got a little Cherokee blood from my daddy, he says. My
mama was full-blooded Choctaw. Ain't seen you before.

I'm from Alabama. I'm about to walk the Trail of Tears back
home. Looking for some adventure.

I thought about doing that one time, he says.

What stopped you?

He downs his drink and orders another. He seems to search
himself as if truth cannot be rushed.

If I knew the answer, he says, I'd know why I'm in *here* right
now.

He raises the new drink to his lips and turns from his stool
to search the smoky room. A blonde with silver dangling earrings
waves from a chair near the pool table. He smiles in surrender.

Think I'd rather walk the Trail of Love, he says, easing from his stool, drink in hand, to walk over and join the blonde.

My name's James, says the bartender. I own this place. Place upstairs too. I got rooms for rent.

James, Cherokee, is around thirty and wears a black beard. He was born and raised in Tahlequah and is one of ten children. His father was self-employed and couldn't produce check stubs to get government help for his family when James was a kid.

It got pretty rough sometimes, says James. We'd go to the dump and gather cornmeal others threw away. Mama made the best cornbread. She knew how to manage too. She'd buy us used Cub Scout clothes. They were made of strong material and would last. I wasn't so much aware of being Indian when I was a boy as I was of being poor. Of course, all that was a long time ago. Now things are much different. I can't complain about business.

It's Labor Day Weekend and the pub is packed. The jukebox rocks and balls on the pool table scatter; players name their holes. A slender and sexy waitress, folded bills between her fingers, hurries about the tables to deliver firewater to Indians and whites alike. It's a Friday night crowd ready to rip.

Another beer? says James.

Not just yet, I say. You going to the powwow this weekend?

No, I never go to those things.

No? I say. Why not?

Well. He laughs. They're okay, but they're like car clubs. Either you're into them or you're not. I got my own powwow here. I got a business to run.

I'm comfortable with James. I like his straightforward manner. But my lungs have had it with the cigarettes. I exit into the fresh night air.

Thunder sounds again in the great distance, but stars still carry on above the treetops. I can breathe freely again and I sit by a stream on the lawn of Northeastern Oklahoma State University. The water rushes over the rocks and the longer I listen the more I forget the crash of pool balls.

I'm not thrilled at the thought of returning to a worn and smelly motel room. I may have been hasty to buy shelter in a strange town. Still, some part of me warms to falling asleep while an old movie plays on TV. Maybe I'm more a member of the modern world than I realize. Just another electronic explorer, climbing mountains in bed.

At Wild River Lounge, I peek in the window to discover a two-story bar and restaurant, jumping with college kids. I'm surprised at my new thirst; I go inside and order a beer. The people here are so blond and white compared to those across the street in Ye Old Pub.

I'm not sure whether to feel sad or to be amused that I'm old enough to be the father of most of the customers. When I was their age, I rode a chopped Harley-Davidson and my friends believed they could change the world.

If you could change anything, I say to a pretty girl who's ordering drinks at the bar, what would you change?

Huh? she says.

No offense, I say. I'm new in town, and just curious about people.

Oh, she says. Let me see. Oh, that's easy. I'd have longer legs. Nice to meet you.

She joins another girl with two guys on the second level. I guess that's the Wild River bragged about outside on the sign: The girl's boyfriend doesn't seem to have any trouble with the length of her legs. His hand eases atop one as he whispers something in her ear. She laughs and pushes him away, but not for long. Her fingertips now crawl over his knee.

I'm halfway through my beer when an Indian in his early

twenties takes a stool next to me. He wears glasses and his shirt is open all the way to his navel. Ted, the owner of the bar, keeps a detective's eye on the man as he makes a phone call.

How are you? I say.

Good, he says. Yourself?

I tell him why I'm in town.

I'm working on a video myself, he says. One about Vietnam Vets. Were you over there?

No, I say. I was lucky. I got a high lottery number in the draft.

The party crowd quiets as two cops make their way to the bar. The man next to me and I watch to see who's caused trouble. I don't get it when they stop behind us.

Could I see you outside? says the first cop.

Why? says the man.

Could we see you? says the second cop. We just want to talk to you.

I doubt if word has gotten around so quickly that the man and I are having such an exciting conversation that the police themselves want to join in.

Can't we talk in here? says the man, fear edging his voice.

*Outside,* says the first cop.

The man leaves with the cops and the party continues. A bit dumbfounded, I raise the beer to my lips.

I told him to stay out of here, says the owner. He's a trouble-maker.

Troublemaker? I say. I don't get it. He seemed harmless enough to me.

You saw how he was dressed, says the owner. Shirt open down to his . . . Thinks he's a producer. Always talking about that video he's making. No, my customers don't want his kind in here.

You're both Cherokee, I say. And you called the cops on him?

So what? he says. Everybody in town's got some Cherokee blood.

I don't know, I say. You could've simply asked him to leave. Shown a little sympathy.

*Sympathy?* he says. Hell, that's what's wrong with America today. Too much sympathy. The guy's a vagabond. He should be locked in a concentration camp. His kind, the poor, fags, and drug addicts, who needs 'em? I hope they all get AIDS and die. Did you know you can get AIDS from glasses?

I wasn't aware of that, I say.

Well, he says. You can. That's why I use plastic cups here at the bar.

Inspired by this gentleman and philosopher, I go outside and spit. I expect to see the cop car. But it's gone, as is the vagabond producer. Perhaps the policemen took him back to the station and handcuffed him while they buttoned his shirt. I hope they got a mug shot of that navel.

I'm glad I'm so tired. I want to fall asleep as my head hits the pillow. But I can't, so I turn on the TV. James Woods is a real hell raiser in the movie *Salvador*. When it ends, I try the dark again. For a reason I can't fully grasp, I'm haunted by the little redheaded girl in the café today. I close my eyes and see her finger, pointing at me. What did she see?

# CHAPTER EIGHT

THE NEXT DAY I'm free of the motel when I go to Northeastern Oklahoma State University to inquire about housing for the rest of the weekend. The housing director is out of town, but his secretary insists that I meet an anthropologist. His name is Dr. Justin Noble, head of Native American Studies at the university. He invites me to stay in his home. He warns me that it's not the Hilton.

It's a one-room log cabin, he says.

Dr. Noble's great-great-grandmother died on the Trail of Tears while giving birth to his great-grandmother. He's also researched his non-Indian blood and traced it back to Russia. He's related to the czar. An expert on the Cherokee, both past and present, it's during one of his stories that I find a clue to the gesture made by the redheaded girl.

Tahlequah is not only Indian, he says. There are different

veins within the community itself. Some still practice sorcery. They believe in *zapping* people.

As he says *zapping,* he gestures with his finger as if it's a gun with a hair trigger; he makes certain to point it away from me. There's no doubt about the gesture, it's the same the little red-headed girl used on me yesterday in the café. I decide, since children mock, she had seen her parents or grandparents practicing such ancient rituals. Or perhaps other children had showed her how to have fun with a toy not sold in K mart.

There's one Cherokee woman, says Dr. Noble, who lives in Muskogee, which is mostly black. She mixes her Indian power with voodoo and sells it there. She's in great demand. On the other hand, there are Indians who help people. They *do medicine.*

I tell myself to put the redheaded girl out of my mind. I refuse to let her finger stir any fears, inviting trouble.

Dr. Noble is as modest as he is generous, for his one room log cabin turns out to be a beautiful place in the woods overlooking a breathtaking valley. It's a log cabin all right, but it's two stories high. I reach my room by climbing a ladder to a bed behind the stone chimney. I couldn't have asked for a cozier place. I feel as safe and welcome here as I do in my cabin back home in the mountains of north Alabama.

I'm a member of the Bird Clan, says Dr. Noble. My bird is the redbird.

Some coincidence, I say. I like birds a lot.

No coincidence, says the anthropologist. Not in my religion. I'd like to make a couple of calls. I know some Indians who would like to talk to you.

While he uses the phone I study old photographs of his Cherokee ancestors, hanging on the wall. I'm struck yet again that their mothers and fathers learned to crawl, walk, dance, make love and cry on the same soil where my father and I grow beans and corn. I have found arrowheads in the area where I plant gourds each summer, but how many generations will it be before wrecked cars are piled as scrap iron to cover the same spot? Don't get me wrong, I can appreciate the wonder of a junkyard. I played in one when I was a kid. It was a blast to drive a car without a motor or tires. Boy, could I take the curves and the hell with parking. I straighten one of the photographs on the wall as Dr. Noble comes from the phone.

That was my friend, Earnie Frost, says Dr. Noble. He's big into his Indian heritage. He's invited us to join him and his family for dinner.

Sounds good, I say, savoring the thought of going to his home for a Cherokee meal.

Do you like Chinese food? he says.

We meet Earnie and his family that night at the Beijing Restaurant. While the food we eat may have evolved on the other side of the globe, Earnie is rooted deeply in his hometown of Tahlequah. He's in his late thirties and wears shoulder-length crow-black hair. A beaded bracelet covers the wrist of an arm leading to wide muscular shoulders. He was in Vietnam.

War hurts, he says. I still have mental wounds from the fighting and I'm afraid that a lot of Cherokee are still under the influence of the war medicine cast by Chief Dragging Canoe in 1792.

I don't follow you, I say.

Dragging Canoe created a spell for war, says Earnie, and all the Cherokee men came under its power. Dragging Canoe was killed before he had time to undo the war medicine. We believe that's why a lot of veterans are suffering today. We don't want to be at war anymore, either with others or within ourselves. We want to be peacemakers, so we've ordered eagle feathers from the federal government to be used in the Eagle Dance in October when the moon is full. We want the dance to release us from the war medicine. We want to be healed.

After the meal, we go to Earnie's home. It's twenty miles from town in the middle of nowhere and a thunderstorm goes crazy; lightning flashes everywhere. He lives in two connecting trailers and rain and wind pound against the metal walls to make it sound as if we'll lift up any moment, to pass Dorothy and the Wicked Witch on her bicycle. But I feel safe *inside* with these people. I'm always touched when someone invites me into his home and means it from the heart. Then, too, I'm a sucker for kids. I like how Earnie and his tall blond wife treat their two boys with tenderness and love.

As we talk about Earnie's concern for his children's future, it's no surprise that we recall that our streams and oceans bubble with pollution as hypodermic needles wash upon our shores.

If the Earth is our mother, I say, how must she feel about what we're doing to her?

Don't worry about her, says Earnie's wife. The Earth was here long before us and it'll be here long after we're gone. It doesn't need us for anything. It's mankind we've got to think about.

Man has lost his vision, says Earnie. Power is what he lives for now. He has forgotten the wisdom of the ducks and geese.

I don't understand, I say.

When they fly in the V, says Earnie, they take turns being the leader. As one tires, the next one comes forward. There's no battle of egos.

I guess my brain has not yet reached the height of a duck or goose. I do not want to be led by anybody but myself. On the other hand, I have no desire to control anyone either. Maybe I just take the easy way out; it's simple to be chief in a one-man tribe.

Earnie has not commented directly on my walk and I can't deny that I seek the blessings of each Cherokee I meet along the way. When he drives Dr. Noble and me back to Tahlequah, he steps beyond all shadows of doubt.

About your journey, he says. Remember the words 'Willow Feather.'

Willow Feather? I say, puzzled.

Yes, he says. I will give you my number. If you have any trouble, just call and say those words or leave them on the answering machine along with your location. We will come to you. Wherever you are.

Words come easy and bullshitters are a dime a dozen, but I've seen enough of Earnie already to know that he's real and will honor his word. I begin to feel that I'm being watched over by a power beyond myself.

Dr. Noble's car is cutting out so Earnie follows us home to the log cabin. When we part he offers his hand. We shake and he pulls our hands up into the air for our shoulders to touch as if brother to brother.

Remember what Jesus said, he says. Get rest. Go gentle as a lamb. And you might want to carry a big sword.

I climb the ladder to my bed behind the chimney and crawl into bed. An owl hoots from a tree; rain falls on the roof. The faint smell of wood smoke lingers in the cabin and it's easy to imagine early Indians sitting around a fire in a cave. Mystery and magic fly with every spark. A car shoots by on the nearby highway and as I fall asleep the Ancient World and the Modern World marry my dreams: I am a hunter seeking new depths of the soul along a Trail marked with telephone poles.

# CHAPTER NINE

I AWAKE IN THE morning to the call of a crow and the fear of disease. What I took in the night, as I turned in half sleep, as a scratch in the wrinkles around my eyes proves in daylight to be a tick. Its head is buried in my skin as if I'm its last meal. There's no pain from the uninvited pig, but it could carry deadly spotted tick fever.

Dr. Noble takes tweezers from his medicine cabinet and pulls the tick from my skin. I sentence the bloodsucker to death down the toilet. I hope I don't awake one morning on the Trail in the woods with four or five ticks digging into my flesh.

I have coffee, says Dr. Noble, putting away the tweezers. Or do you prefer tea?

I prefer conversation for breakfast and learn that Dr. Noble, in his fifties, is about to adopt a man of twenty-five. He is obligated to do this since the fatherless Indian asked him; it is a

Cherokee tradition. The ceremony is in two days by a river. The young man will remove his clothes and throw them into the water, where they will float away like old skin. As the new father, Dr. Noble will furnish new clothes while a medicine man, Pat Moss, conducts a secret ritual. For his services, he will receive a twist of tobacco and two and one half yards of cloth, along with some good old American cash. When Dr. Noble dies, he must also tell his ancestors in the other world that the adopted son will one day join them. He must inform the birds as well.

I once had a girlfriend, says Dr. Noble, who could become an owl.

When I lived in New Orleans for eight years, I had a lover who could become a cat. I loved to ease my fingers through her fur and become a snake. Somewhere along the way we lost the magic and I wouldn't dare say what we then became.

I hope you have a safe journey, says Dr. Noble as I prepare to leave. I couldn't march alone like you.

Thanks for everything, I say. Talk to the birds for me. Ask them to keep me company along the way.

I strap on the backpack and walk the Trail down Highway 62. I'm almost out of Tahlequah when an old Indian, hobbling with a cane, stops me. He's thin and his wrinkled face is weathered with stories. His eyes seem to see something I don't as he leans on the cane and into my face.

Walking the Trail? he says.

Yes, I say, wondering how he knows.

Soul Harbor, he says. You be on the lookout for Soul Harbor. They'll put you up and feed you.

Soul Harbor, I say.

He nods as if trying to tell me something more with his eyes. I gather that he's referring to a shelter for the homeless. Or is he trying to tell me something else? I've been in Tahlequah only four days, but already time and space are taking on new dimensions. I was zapped by a child practicing sorcery. I was the house guest of an anthropologist whose past girlfriend could become an owl and I was given the code word—Willow Feather—by a member of a Cherokee secret society. Now a total stranger, looming out of nowhere like a myth come alive, insists that I look for Soul Harbor. Definitely not short on intrigue, I push on down the Trail and Tahlequah disappears around the bend.

Highway 62 winds eastward up and down rolling hills where creeks meander among oaks and pastures. Cattle graze and horses kick and run. Just enough mist fills the air to soften and cool a sometimes brutal sun. Blue jays call among the leaves while a crow sits alone in a dead tree to squawk his ancient song.

I sink my teeth into a red apple as I march farther into this dream come true. I have no time clock to rattle a ball and chain by day and I have no alarm clock to darken my nights with dread. I have no boss looking over my shoulder and no fellow workers to step around. I have no wife to explain myself to and no bill collectors at my door. I'm in my element doing what I do best, feeling free.

I finish the apple and offer the core to a horse. He's tempted, but slow to trust a stranger. When he finally takes it, his giant teeth make my fingers jerk away as fast as a striking rattlesnake.

Going on a hike? says a kid on a bicycle, slowing beside me.

Yeah, I say. All the way to Alabama.

Wow! That'll take you a year.

No, I say. Just a few months at most.

I wish I was going, he says. I don't like school. You gonna kill your food?

Yep. Gonna use a bow and arrow. If I get caught in the mountains when it snows, I'll have to kill a bear for a coat and live in a cave till spring comes.

Aaah, he says. You ain't gonna do that. *Are* you?

No, I say. Just playing. I'll get food from grocery stores and eat in cafés along the way. I might do a little fishing. What's in your bag?

Nintendo game. I just got it from a friend. Mister, can I have your autograph?

I don't feel like I've accomplished anything in my life to make my autograph worth anything, and this kid's request melts my heart.

Sure, I say. Want me to write you a big check while I'm at it?

Aaah, he laughs. You're goofy.

I write my name on his paper bag and he pedals away. I feel like a kid myself as he disappears around the bend, his bagged Nintendo game swinging back and forth beneath his fingers gripping the handlebar.

After walking ten miles the fifty-pound pack feels like a hundred pounds. My feet are burning and two blisters have homesteaded between my toes. The mist has stopped and the sun beats down. If I could sell my sweat by the cupful, I'd be a rich man. Some of it runs down my cheeks and into my mouth. I taste the salt and past lovers come to mind. How *they* tasted. How they used their tongues. How drops of sweat dripped from my face onto their lips and breasts.

I stop and take off the pack. I unzip the top compartment and lift the canteen to my lips. I had forgotten just how wonderful water can be. I pause a few seconds between mouthfuls to feel the cool run down my throat and let anticipation build for the next drink. I get lost, however, in the sensations and drink almost all the water before I realize it.

The sergeant within me slaps the pack on my back again and I have six more miles to walk to Proctor, where Dub has offered me a place to camp. The two blisters seem to grow with each step and they're like having two lighted cigarettes in my shoes. I'm disgusted with myself for not having walked with the pack before the trip to toughen my feet. This lack of foresight is the product of lifting weights for twenty-seven years. I bought my own propaganda and believe I can do anything requiring muscle. *Faster than a speeding bullet. Able to leap tall buildings in a single bound.* By the time I arrive in Proctor I'm doing good to lift one foot in front of the other. The two blisters now feel so big that I may have to name them. My water ran out over an hour ago and my pack—it thinks I don't know this—is actually an alien that converts mileage into iron. I'm now walking down the road with a truck strapped to my back.

Proctor has only one store and a post office. Eight or ten small country houses are scattered among trees. Twelve to fifteen hummingbirds dart about two feeders, hanging in front of the store's window. I've never seen so many tiny feathered acrobats at one time. They seem to twirl and flip to a music of their own. Our Creator, whatever His name, must've conceived their gentle humming beauty after making love. They're a perfect *welcome* to Proctor Grocery.

# CHAPTER TEN

I LEAVE MY pack by the door and go into the store, to find Everett Kendel seated at a table with a deck of cards. He's seventy-seven and the locals call him the mayor of Proctor. He's as thin as a broomstick and has a smile that could sell a bull to a China shop. He holds a flyswatter and demonstrates his skill from time to time; excuse those drops of blood on the table.

Yeah, he says. I was born and raised right here in Proctor. After the Indians settled here, my folks came. Why, just shake any bush and a Kendel will run out.

This is the first general store I've been to in years and I'm happy to learn sandwiches are made to order. I down a soft drink as the lady owner slices smoked turkey. I'm so tired and thankful to have the first day behind me that I'm content just to sit and be nothing more than two ears.

Now, I ain't got no Indian blood myself, says the mayor, trying in vain to hit a fly in midair. But I grew up with the Cherokee. Never will forget the first time I saw one. He carried a pistol and made this white man dance by shooting at his feet, just like you see in the movies. That man was a *fast* dancer too. Some of them didn't speak much English when I was boy. They taught me some of their language. One taught me how to do the Snake Dance and the Stomp Dance. He was an old Indian and smoked a pipe. He could blow smoke rings big enough to swallow a dog.

The sandwiches, complete with tomatoes and lettuce, are so thick with sliced turkey that I can barely get them in my mouth. I decide it'll be easier if I eat only one at a time. I have to ask again when the owner says they're only a dollar apiece.

I live just down that dirt road there, says the mayor. Live all alone, except for my dog. Got an extra bed, if you'd like to stay there.

The food and a little rest now begin to pull my body back together and the romance of the journey once more spreads its wings. Here I am, a total stranger, invited to make myself at home. I got a real soft spot for old men and women, and as the mayor looks into my eyes I see that he needs company.

How about if I come visit, I say, after I pitch my tent?

I'll be there, says the mayor, springing from his chair to swing the flyswatter like only a pro knows how. *There,* he brags, I showed the little devil.

My feet hurt like hell as I go outside and slip into the pack. Dub lives across the road next to the post office, run by his wife. I tell her who I am, and start to explain why I'm there.

He told me, she says. He's not back from his mail route, but you're sure welcome.

I find a spot in the grass to pitch my nylon two-man tent. I found it on the same radio Trade Line where I found the army tent I'm using to cover the sweatlodge. I had to dial the show several times before I got on, right after the woman who wanted to sell a car without a motor.

Otherwise, she had said, it's a good running old car.

It's an unwritten law in Alabama that everything has to have a story before you can sell it. The nylon tent was no exception. When I went to see it, the man had it rolled out on his front yard. I walked around it like a horse trader, searching for bad teeth.

How long you had it? I asked.

A year, he said. No, closer to two.

How much?

Eight dollars, he said.

The price was just right. But maybe too right. I had to dig deeper. He could have been a professional used tent salesman, passing himself off as a good old boy.

It's leakproof?

No, he said. But it's water resistant.

His genuine voice and frankness almost convinced me. But why would a man want to sell a tent for only eight bucks? I continued to circle the tent a time or two more before I got down on its level to give it the finger test. I figured if I stalled long enough, he would feel compelled to spill his guts. Finally, he confessed.

I ain't gonna use it no more, he said. I took it down into the canyon to camp and tripped over a rattlesnake as big around as my leg. I chopped its head off with an axe.

So, it was a snake tent, cursed to call the meanest and most deadly of all reptiles. Only a man who was intrigued by a creature able to swallow an entire rabbit at once would have considered making this tent his home.

I'll take it, I said.

* * *

Once I have the tent pitched, I drag my pack inside and
inflate a sleeping pad. I unroll my sleeping bag and blow up a
plastic pillow. It's two or three hours before dark, but I've got to
get some rest. First, however, I remove my shoes and socks to
perform fingernail-clipper surgery on the two blisters. I swear
right here and now, and I'll put it in blood, that I'll never ever
again look down on my feet like second-class citizens to only be
walked on. I massage them and the pain fades. For a few seconds.

It's almost sundown when I come from resting in the tent.
I'm on the way to the mayor's house when I spot Dub at the
store; he's pumping gas into his truck.

Glad you made it, he says. I got to go tend to some cattle, but
I'll be back in a bit. I got something for you.

He fishes into his pocket and removes something that looks
like a chestnut. I put it to my nose and sniff. Tree bark comes to
mind.

It's a buckeye, he says. First one I ever found growing in
these parts.

The gift may be for good luck on my trip. But I suspect he
means for me to use it in a burial ritual I have planned back in
Alabama. I want to gather items along the way and bury them
near my cabin in honor of the Indians who died before and
during the Trail of Tears. I slide the buckeye into my pocket and
follow the dirt road beside the store.

There's at least one good reason for living in Oklahoma, and
that's the sunsets. They can trick a man who is down, into looking up. Pinks and blues swirl together in slow motion, as if a new
species is being created before my very eyes. A breeze rustles the
leaves and I take a deep breath to get a faint hint of autumn. I

wouldn't trade who I am or how I feel just now with anybody on the face of the earth.

My body, however, begins to ache again when my mind comes from the sunset. My feet are so sore that it takes all I can do not to walk like a duck as I pass four kids playing softball in front of a house. I can't swear that the boy at bat doesn't say *quack* to the pitcher.

I'm relieved when the dirt road curves to the right and I disappear behind another house. I can now waddle to my heart's content.

On my left rots a factory which once canned tomatoes and beans. Back in its heyday it filled the workers' pockets with enough cash to keep three whole stores going. The town of Proctor was five hundred strong back then. Only a hundred or so remain now. I would go nuts working in a factory, but the crumbling building makes me sad for those who had to move to the cities to find work. I fear the kids didn't have trees to climb or creeks to jump as they grew. Without such landmarks in nature, I wonder if we don't suffer the loss of something as indescribable but vital as love.

Between the factory and the mayor's house is a pond, and a frog jumps as I approach. It creates a small splash and a dog begins to bark at the mayor's screen door.

You shut up now, says the mayor. His name is Benny. He won't bite. Come on in, son.

The dog smells me and lets me pass. I take a seat on the couch and pretend not to notice that part of the ceiling is about ready to collapse. A rusty horseshoe hangs over the door to the kitchen.

For good luck? I say.

Yeah, he says. But I'll tell you, son, I ain't had all good luck.

The cancer got me. The doctors say they got it all though. Got a sister who's ninety-five. She lives in a nursing home.

Benny wags his tail, deciding I'm okay. He sticks his head against my leg and I pet him.

Did I tell you Jesse James had his hideout around here? says the mayor. Well, he did and the law could've caught the sun itself before they got old Jesse James. These hills are filled with hiding spots. Up there you got Turkey Holler, and over that way you got Pumpkin Holler. Come back around over this way and you end up in Crazy Holler. You like football?

The TV has been on since I arrived, and the quarterback is now being blitzed. With some fancy footwork, however, he manages to fire a pass for a thirty-yard reception. As night falls I sit with the old man and his dog as if our very lives depend on the outcome of this game on TV. At first, I feel a little cheated, for I want to pick his brain to hear stories that led him to this very spot where he'll die, beside a pond and a ghost factory. But when I let go of my desires, I see in the old man's eyes that he's happy simply to have someone sit with him. I don't have to talk or have money or dress a certain way. All I have to do is just sit and be, while the TV plays. I'm not sure if he's reached such a point of wisdom or if his life is just that empty. Either way, he makes me feel important for giving so little.

He should've had that pass, says the mayor.

It was right in his hands, I say. Benny could've caught that pass.

When the football game ends, the mayor is almost asleep in his chair while Benny lazes at his feet. I'm so tired that I don't want to move, but I say good night and walk back to my tent. I crawl inside and take off all my clothes except for underwear. I've never been more aware of my skin. It's slowly sinking in just how vulnerable I am without walls to protect me at night. But it's something more than basic shelter I'm sensing. I'm now exposed to people in a way I've never been before. Whether I like it or not, I will feel a certain amount of what they feel, be it joy or sadness. It's one thing to have big muscles and lift heavy weights. It's another to be strong where it really counts.

I slide into my sleeping bag and zip it up. I lay my head on the small inflated pillow. The tent, my most outer layer of skin, flaps in the wind; the earth's energy never stops. An occasional car or truck comes down the road, and through the nylon they are glowing eyes, which get bigger and bigger till they vanish into red dots.

Only ten feet from my tent stands a TV dish, catching signals across the globe. A small light flickers in Dub's house and I gather they watch some show. With my body against the earth in the very path where the Cherokee marched with Death, my mind gropes to tell me something. The message twists and turns, trying to be born. It's not easy to be a midwife to the soul.

I'm too tired, or too dense, to grasp what stirs within concerning the TV dish, earth, and man. *Go to sleep,* I tell myself, *get some rest.*

A whippoorwill calls as I pray for protection and put my arm around my backpack. At least, it doesn't snore.

# CHAPTER ELEVEN

THE MAYOR USUALLY arrives at Proctor Grocery, along with the acrobatic hummingbirds, several minutes before the door opens at seven, but I'm the first one here today and I order a couple more of the famous turkey sandwiches for breakfast. The coffee's free, but donations are accepted if you're inspired. Just drop the silver in the cup next to the one with the Sweet'n Low.

School kids hurry in and out to grab a bag of potato chips or a candy bar to lighten the classroom load, and I'm not embarrassed for them to see me walk today; my feet are fine and itching to travel. I just might jump a log or two for the hell of it. If the notion strikes me, I might even climb a tree.

By the time the owner has my sandwiches made, the mayor arrives to warm his chair and shuffle the cards. The trusty flyswatter isn't far away.

How'd the ground sleep last night? asks the mayor.

Well, I say. It was softer than a bed of nails.

The school bus stops and the kids moan as they're sucked on board. I'm finishing my last sandwich when the owner makes it clear my chair has her name on it. Two others have arrived, including a Choctaw. Stand back, ladies and gentlemen, it's time for the day's card game to burn a hole in the table.

You leaving already? says the mayor as he deals.

I sometimes like to say good-bye when people are doing what they enjoy. It leaves a pretty picture in my mind.

I put on my pack and start down the road, but I turn to see the hummingbird show one more time. As the birds dart about I see into the future and they disappear: It's winter now and snow falls on their empty feeders. The mayor, rubbing his wrinkled old hands together, waits alone before the morning's locked door.

Last night's hint of autumn lingers in today's breeze. Dew covers spiderwebs, like lace for a woman's most delicate secrets. Sumac is already turning red and a few poplar leaves promise rare yellows.

A farmer, wiping his neck with a red handkerchief, burns a pile of brush. The smoke rises through the trees and drifts over the barn. A rooster scratches by the giant back tire of an old tractor, just rusting away. Two white pigeons fly from the barn loft and seem to float upon the smoke for a second or two before they disappear beyond a TV antenna.

A woman, who I take to be the farmer's wife, hangs clothes on a line stretched between two apple trees. Twenty or thirty apples are scattered on the ground, and the branches are so loaded that they hang earthward as if ready to break and get it over with.

Could I buy an apple? I say.

The woman takes a clothespin from her mouth and gives me

a closer going over. She's in her fifties and her eyes dart to the field where the farmer pokes the fire.

Take a couple, she says. There's no charge.

Thanks, I say. How about him?

What? she says.

I show the worm hole in the apple.

No. She finally smiles. He's free too. Get you another one. Half of them just lay there and rot anyway.

Her Indian eyes dart once again to her husband, by the fire some seventy or eighty yards away. He returns my wave, but I see no smile and think it best to move on.

Be careful about those cars, she says. Some of them don't know the difference between people and armadillos.

She's simply being thoughtful, but I don't like having my nose rubbed in dead animals. The road is lined with flattened armadillos; it looks like a sport where drivers burn full tanks in the night just to run them down. Some of the kills are fresh while others are now only skeletons, bleached by the sun. I can't walk more than half a mile before the smell of death grabs me in the building heat.

I save the two apples till I come to an oak where the air is fresh and the shade is cool. I slip from the load and lean my back against the massive trunk. It's good to rest, but I'm troubled.

I've walked almost fifteen miles today and I was naive to think my feet would toughen overnight. Two new blisters have moved in and I remove my shoes and socks to pop them. I open my canteen and pour water over my swollen and burning flesh. It disturbs me that I now question why I'm here and what I'm doing. Can I really make it all the way back home?

It's a half mile back to where the farmer burns the brush; the smoke streams high overhead. A crow flies over it and I hurry to pull my crow caller from my pocket. I squawk four or five times and the bird finally changes the course of his flight in my direction. I hide behind the oak and call again; he dares to answer. It may not be a telegram from American Sweepstakes, but, hey, it's contact with another living creature, and I'm not so sure that birds aren't worth more than money.

A second crow now appears out of nowhere and I squawk as if a party is about to happen. A third and fourth crow join the circle and the treetops swarm with excitement. I can't deny a little pride in calling such a meeting to order, and damned if I don't find it giving me my second wind.

At the intersection of 59 and 62 at Westville, Oklahoma, I limp into a convenience store. Aaah, an air conditioner.

You walking too? says an Indian woman of about thirty, seated at a booth by the window.

Walking, crawling, whatever, I say, taking a booth next to hers.

I walked two miles to here, she says. My car wouldn't start today. You not got a car?

Yes, I say. It's parked down the road about eight hundred and fifty miles. I'm walking the Trail of Tears.

That *is* you, says a man, paying the cashier. I read about you in the paper.

The *Daily Oklahoman* did a story with my picture that came out yesterday. This is the first person to recognize me and I feel just a bit exposed and vulnerable.

You're going to *walk* all that distance? the man continues. Oh, there's some mean people in the world. Be careful you don't get killed sleeping in that tent.

That thought'll help me rest at night, I say.

Oh, well, says the man. You know what I mean. People are

just so crazy today. Didn't used to be that way. People cared about each other.

I've met good people so far, I say.

Now people would just as soon shoot you as look at you, says the man. You carrying a gun?

No.

I'd carry *me* a gun, says the man. I can tell you that much right now.

Why don't you come with me? I ask. You can walk in front of me with a pistol.

He opens his mouth to say something, but only an awkward laugh comes out as he leaves the store. I take off my hat and place it on the table.

Should I order the fish, I say, or the chicken?

The fish, says the Indian woman, whose name is Virginia. The chicken's not very good.

I get the fish and return to my booth. It would make a great meal for Marines in basic training. It chews like it's been battered with leather. I don't really care though. It's filling and it's cool in here. I like watching strangers come and go with milk or eggs or whatever as Virginia and I chew the fat.

I never went to a regular doctor, she tells me, till I was almost grown. Mama always took me to this old medicine woman. She'd give me teas or spit tobacco juice on me and say stuff in Cherokee. It worked too. One time I got this big cut on my leg and it would've taken thirty stitches to sew it up. She just spit on it and it healed like new.

What are you doing in here? I ask.

Waiting on my ride to work, she says. That's why I keep looking out the window. I work at a greeting-card company in the next town. It's not so bad, but the job I had before it was horrible. I worked in a chicken plant. Did it all too. Cutting, gutting, hanging. It was real messy. I can work on cars too. My husband makes me. I have to be a woman and a man. I don't care. I'm not like those Indians who live on a reservation. All they do is sit around all day. I wouldn't mind trying it though.

Virginia isn't what society would call a knockout. *Cosmopolitan* will never do a story on her poise and grace. She'll never host the *Today* show with Bryant Gumbel. But, for me, somewhere between the chickens she gutted and the tobacco that was spit on her, is a beauty.

Mind if I take your picture? I say.

*Mine?* she says, looking behind her to make certain I'm talking to her. Why do you want to take a picture of me?

You have an interesting face, I say.

Nobody ever asked to take my picture before, she says, pushing hair from her eyes. You sure?

Her humility only adds to her beauty and I feel a bit guilty about my own vanity. How many millions of people in America must go through their entire lives and never feel unique or special because, in part, we so value the architecture of bones and skin. It's sometimes those with plain faces that have the most inviting eyes. They're so hungry and honored that someone will notice.

There's a place for you to camp just down the road a few miles, says Virginia. It's a church surrounded by woods. It was brought out from Georgia on the Trail of Tears. That's what it's called the Trail of Tears Church.

Wait a minute, I say. You're telling me they brought a whole church out here in 1838?

Well, she says. That's what I've been told.

# CHAPTER TWELVE

I LIKE IT when I change from Route 62 East to Route 59 North outside the store; it spells progress. When I arrive at the church an hour later, it's like a scene Norman Rockwell might've painted. A white wooden church with a steeple faces the east where an old cemetery waits across the road. A field stretches to the right of the building, while woods are thick on the left. Between the woods and the church is a green yard with a giant oak. And, just like Virginia said, written across the top of the building is:

OLD BAPTIST MISSION CHURCH
Brought from Georgia on the Trail of Tears in 1838

The oak sets far from the road and I couldn't have asked for a better spot to camp. I pitch my tent facing the east so that I can behold the sunrise and wonder at the moon over wide open fields beyond the cemetery. A train track, snaking through the countryside, only adds to the beauty. I'm so happy with this spot, people driving by can think I'm a down-and-out hobo, for all I care.

I take off my shoes and socks and walk through the grass to let it tickle my toes. My feet, just out of jail on a bum rap, cry freedom. Earlier today, how could I have doubted myself and the walk? I had bought a six-pack of cold beer back at the store, and now I open a can as I sit to lean against the oak. My whole body aches, but my mind is at peace. I had forgotten just how good you can feel after doing hard labor all day.

When I head for the church door, I discover I'm not alone. A slick blacksnake, over three feet long, crawls over the concrete landing as if it follows a path only it can see. Its lightning-fast tongue shoots in and out of its mouth as it butts its head against the underside of the raised door. When it senses my presence, it slides its head into a hole under the church. The building seems to suck it into another world, its body becoming only a tail and then nothing but the blackness of the hole behind green grass.

I enter the church and the smell of pine brings me back to other country churches I recall from childhood. *Do you walk with the lamb or the lion? Is your heart filled with love or hate? If you died today, would you fly away on the wings of a dove or would you swell in the belly of a beast?* I lift a hymn book and thumb through the pages. I stop on "The Rock of Ages," where someone has written in pencil: Can I see you tonight? Underneath is written: Daddy won't let me. How about tomorrow after school?

A newspaper article is framed behind glass on the wall: Four or five beams in the building were brought from a church in Georgia in 1838 on the Death March. Another article speaks of a wagon train that passed through here last year. One man, a trucker, was so taken with the travelers that he jumped his job and joined them. Yes, sir, a Gypsy is my kind of man. Eat, drink, and be merry, for tomorrow you might wonder why the hell you didn't.

A picture of Jesus, forever looking upward, hangs near the pulpit. I go to it and turn to face the empty pews. For a fleeting second they come alive with Indians from 150 years ago on the Trail of Tears. They are worn and dirty and their clothes are torn. The floor is spotted with blood where shoeless feet have walked. An old woman without teeth holds her husband's head in her lap. His eyes are closed; he is trembling. She strokes his hair as her frail body gently rocks back and forth, back and forth.

Sadness and fear collide within me. I begin to sweat and my heart pounds as a chant, no louder than a whisper, rises from my gut and through my chest to come from my mouth. The chant becomes louder and one of the Indians begins to chant with me. One by one, all the Indians begin to chant till the church is so filled with the pulsation of human spirits that the windows themselves vibrate as if pushed by the wind of an approaching storm. The old man, shaking in his wife's lap, opens his eyes for the first time and sees into me with such wisdom that I no longer have a structure of muscle and blood and bone. I am only a field of energy, a state of feelings, quivering in air to send sound about the walls and the floor and the ceiling as the old man's eyes seem to come closer and closer—

A small crash against the window brings me back to *this* world. The old man and the other Indians have vanished. I stop chanting and see a bird fly away from the window it just crashed into. I become anxious that a church member might've stopped to investigate my tent and heard me chanting, singing a song that isn't in the hymn book.

I approach the exit. A stranger, listening just beyond the

door, might swear I'm crazy. What could I say in my defense? How could I explain what I feel and see?

I open the door and I'm relieved that no one waits outside. I go down the steps where the slick blacksnake disappeared into the grass. The redbird that crashed into the window now sits in the oak above my tent. He looks rather stunned as the sun begins to set.

A rabbit eating grass at the edge of the woods near the tent spots me and runs for shelter. Its white cotton tail fades into the brush and the dry leaves rustle beneath its feet.

I cross the road to walk into the cemetery. I find the site where the Cherokee Jesse Bushyhead, the church's founder, is buried. Born in what is now Cleveland, Tennessee—sixty miles north of my cabin—he had studied English and became an ordained Baptist minister in 1830. His religion had one edge over the others for appealing to the Cherokee: They liked the idea of being baptized in a creek or river, for such a ritual had been used by the shaman for hundreds of years and was referred to as *going to water,* to help purify a man's spirit.

I go back to the tent and crawl inside to rest. A truck arrives and a man steps out. I'm anxious that he may want to know who I am and why I've invited myself to camp on this land. I quickly give him the dime tour of my walk.

Well, he says, thrusting posthole diggers into the ground. That's some chore you got mapped out.

The ground is so hard that the diggers barely make a dent; red dust flies. He tries again without much better luck. The earth just doesn't want to give in.

Want some help? I say, peeking from the tent's net door.

He's digging four holes to hold an iron frame for children's swings. They will face the cemetery as they swing back and forth to the chain's squeaking song.

No, says the digger, wiping sweat from his forehead. I'll get it. You go ahead and rest.

I lie back down, and though I don't know this stranger, it's comforting that he's here. The rhythm of his tool hitting the ground puts me to sleep.

I awake when his truck pulls from the churchyard. It's almost dark now and I come from the tent to relieve myself before turning in for the night. The moon is already out and the cemetery has become ghostly. But not in a way that frightens. Rather, it intrigues me.

I'm about to crawl back into the tent when a truck slows to pull into the yard. I assume it's the worker, that he forgot something. But it's not him.

Some guy comes from a van with a red Irish setter. The dog runs to the edge of the woods; he smells where the rabbit ran. Giving up on that, the dog runs to jump up on me.

Come here, Red, shouts the man. Leave him alone.

It's okay, I say as saliva pours from the dog's mouth onto my hand. How you doing?

I'm tired, he says. Been driving all day. I'm headed down to Texas to see some friends.

They're not cold, I say, but I have some beer, if you'd like one. It goes down just the same.

Let's have one of mine, he says. They're cold.

I'm all up for that cold one and he introduces himself as Bob. But his friends call him Hank because he looks a lot like Hank Williams.

I pick the guitar a little, says Hank. But I can't sing worth a shit. I thought I could, till I heard myself on a tape recorder. That was a real kick in the ass.

Hank is forty-four and wears a beard. Faded jeans and cowboy boots get the lower half. His sweatshirt with the sleeves cut out is white with a picture of Mick Jagger painted on the back; his singing lips stretch from one side of the shirt to the other.

Eh, he says. Some girl I used to date in Chicago did this shirt for me. Don't know why I keep hanging on to it. She turned out to be a real bloodsucker. Came home from work one day and she had left with my stereo, TV, and clock radio. What made it so bad was that I didn't get any hint it was coming. Me, I was stupid enough to be in love with her. Hell, I guess I still love her. She had a coke problem, but I didn't know it till it was too late. I tried to help her. Well, they say you learn from your experiences. Ain't that right, Red?

We're sitting in the grass under the oak and the Irish setter lies nearby. He wags his tail and moans when Hank rubs his head.

Hank lives part-time in his van, equipped with a bed, ice box, and butane stove. A chest of drawers is bolted to one wall, while a small closet is built into the other. He grew up near Austin. His father was a drunk and left him and his two brothers with his mother when he was eight. He hasn't heard from him since.

I went to a couple of meetings, he says, for children of alcoholics. I had a lot I wanted to deal with. Stuff that was bottled up inside. But after a couple of meetings I said the devil with it. I knew I hated the son-of-a-bitch. How many times can you say that and get anything new out of it? Your father still alive?

Yeah, I say. We're close.

You're lucky, he says, rubbing behind the dog's ears. I haven't seen my brothers or my mother in five years. That's why I'm going home. Mother's in the hospital. My brother wouldn't tell me what it is. I'm scared. All this time I been pissing my life away. I haven't even written her or talked to her in six months.

The night grows darker and the moon reflects on the tomb-

stones across the road. When Hank was in high school, he and
two other boys and one girl took a dare on a Friday night to dig
up a grave. They did it and thought they were real bad asses till
Hank found out that the man they unearthed was the father of his
math teacher, who was so disturbed that she missed a few days of
school; Hank felt like hell.

She was a good person, he says. I couldn't sleep till I went to
the preacher of the church. I told him everything and I figured
he'd call the cops. But he didn't. He had me go to the man's grave
and ask forgiveness. I don't know if I even believe in life after
death, but I was a ton lighter after that. I guess I've about wore
your ear out. I don't usually talk so much, but with Mother in the
hospital and all . . . I think it's good what you're doing for the
Indians.

It's not only for them, I say. I need it for myself. It'll give me
a chance to do some soul-searching. Maybe help pull me through
the mid-life crisis.

Maybe that's what I'm going through, he says, crushing his
beer can. Look how easy this thing bends. I hate aluminum.
Plastic too. Well, it's good for pipes though. I do plumbing when
I have to. I don't really like it.

I like Hank and wish he didn't have to go. He says he'll be
on the lookout for me when he goes back to Chicago. But I accept
that I'll probably never see him and Red again as they crawl into
the van.

I hope your mother's okay, I say.

Yeah, he says, getting a bit choked up. I hope so too. Don't
take any wooden Indians.

I'll remember, I say.

He starts the van and pulls from the churchyard. He and Red
disappear down the road and I'm left alone. On one hand, I feel
lucky to be meeting so many people. On the other hand, it hurts
to start getting close to somebody and see him vanish.

# CHAPTER THIRTEEN

I HAVEN'T SEEN a sunrise in over a year, and I awake to the very beginning of an orange sun that is so brilliant and powerful I can almost swear a volcano is being born just a mile or two to the east. My mind is clear from the night's deep sleep and my rested body is charged with new energy. I ponder the Master Fire getting bigger and bigger by the second. Then I see the Earth going around the Sun and the Moon going around the Earth as the whole galaxy soars among the stars. A breeze against my naked flesh sends a chill down my spine and over my entire body and I'm caught once again in the thrill of being part of it all.

I take a couple of shirts and a sweater from my pack to lighten my load. I put them in a box in the church and write a note, thanking the members for a place to sleep.

The place where the tick buried his head in the wrinkles

around my right eye seems to have healed, but a couple of miles down the road this morning I discover I have new guests: Chiggers chew my stomach and thighs.

Maybe ya'll would like some ketchup or hot sauce? I say. How about something to drink? No, no, it would be no trouble at all. Please, I insist.

I'm sure I look like a monkey with a backpack by the way I scratch. I try to turn the nagging pain into a game and see if I can make it to the next telephone pole without attacking myself. Halfway there I become a slave to passion and scratch as if inventing a new sport, riveting with speed and technique. Ah, these great moments in history.

The Trail is so damn thick in spots with grasshoppers that they look like swarms of locusts. They land on my jeans and shirt, and create tiny but distinct pulling sensations as they fly back into tall sun-baked weeds. From their mouths drips a juice the color of tobacco. As a kid, I believed that if they spit in your eyes you'd go blind, just like that. Boy, did a sharp fishhook show them who was boss.

A hundred yards from the road, out in a field, a dead cow is torn apart by eleven buzzards. As I get closer, three of the giant birds fly away. Then four more fly; finally only one is left. It continues to peck away at the rotting flesh as if it could care less about me. When I pass, two more of the birds return, their massive wings creating a small cloud of red dust.

Some Indians did not view the buzzard as a sign of death. On the contrary, they saw it as an omen of healing because it could eat the diseased without worry of infection.

I stop at a creek to rest and I'm amazed at how clear the water is. A bass, about a foot long, darts under the bridge. The head of a snake rises from the water. No, it's a turtle swimming upstream, followed by a second and then a third. I've never seen anything like it. They appear to play follow-the-leader. As the first one goes down so do the next two, all in a single straight line. The leader surfaces and his small navy does the same.

Watching the turtles playing in the creek reminds me of a story the Cherokee used to tell long ago. The lowly turtle could once whistle, and he loved to dazzle the birds and animals with his songs. The quail asked to borrow his whistle one day. The kindhearted turtle agreed and the quail soared to the top of a tree, the whistle forever out of reach. The turtle was so ashamed that from that day forth he hid in his box when a human approached.

It's noon and almost 100 degrees. The water down below looks perfect for soaking my baked feet; I start toward it. But as I take the second step down the bank I'm jolted by what I find. Three hypodermic needles are scattered in the grass and it pisses me off. I'd like to punch the pitiful guy who tossed them from his car. For all I know they're infected with the AIDS virus and I could've stepped on one.

I hurry back up the bank and onto the road. What if some kids find those needles and get stuck? Maybe I should go back and bury them, but I don't. I'm still so damned pissed that I can't see straight. I tend to think of addicts being in the cities, but what a joke. Now we have to watch our every step when we go for a walk in the country.

It's unusual for me to get mad, but I can't kick this rage. I walk as fast as I can. Even the blue jays and the crows don't lift me from the mud. I kick a beer can six feet into the air and spit when I spot yet another paper bag from McDonald's. A styrofoam cup here, a plastic diaper there. Cigarette wrappers by the dozen. Rubbers for safe sex. Soft drink cans by the truckload.

That afternoon I arrive in Siloam Springs, Arkansas, and I haven't shaved or bathed in three days. I check on a motel room. The owner has her hair in curlers and unlocks the door for my inspection. It's twenty-one dollars a night, and even chicken fighters might give a second thought to letting their prize roosters sleep here. We're talking Dump City.

Thanks for showing me, I say. I think I'll take a rain check. Is John Brown University nearby?

Down that way, she snaps. Three blocks.

I decide I've got nothing to lose but a little pride if I ask about housing for the night from the college. The campus is set on rolling hills with trees and manicured lawns. Better than that, it's crawling with sensuous college girls. I consider it a great feat of strength just to keep my eyes in my head. Now if I can master control of my hands and stop slobbering, I might be able to present myself as a humble pilgrim.

Managing, somehow, not to run headfirst into any trees while eyeing the young ladies, I find the admissions office. When I enter the lobby with my pack and crow feather sticking from my sweat-stained hat, the receptionist isn't sure how to respond.

Is it too late to sign up for the survival course? I say.

Uh, well . . . I, she says.

I tell her what I'm doing.

I don't think it'll be a problem, she says. There's a few empty rooms in the dorm. But I can't make that decision. My boss is out to lunch right now.

I leave my pack with her and start out to find a café. I haven't eaten since yesterday and I'm starved. I'm heading across the admissions office lawn when someone hurries from the building.

Wait a minute, shouts a plump man in his early twenties. I overheard your conversation. Could I take you to lunch as a guest of the university?

What a question.

That would be great, I say, offering my hand.

His name is Richard Ruiz. A Mexican-American, he went to school here at John Brown and stayed on to work as a recruiter. When he returns from the admissions office with a couple of meal tickets, we head for the cafeteria.

I'll have to ask you to remove your hat, says Richard, as we get in line for food. Did you know this was a Christian college?

No, I say, becoming a bit paranoid that red lights will flash and bells will ring at any second. Well, think about it: For all I know, in this high-tech age of lasers and electronic spying devices, they could have an erection detector or a lust meter installed over the salad bar or in the wall next to where we sit to eat. If I could only slap myself without drawing attention, I might get my mind off the surrounding young ladies. I could say a fly landed on my face, but it might, on second thought, appear a bit extreme. No, there's no way around it. I've just got to deal with my passion like a real man; I'll suppress it and try to carry on a serious conversation. If smoke starts coming from my ears, I'll swear I have no idea what's going on. Maybe something I ate.

Were you born in Mexico? I ask.

No, says Richard, who's really a nice guy and trying to make my walk something special. But my father was. He was born in an adobe shack in Nuevo Laredo, Mexico. He was a migrant worker and so were his parents. My going to college has been a big deal for my family. For three generations we've been migrant workers. I began picking tomatoes when I was six.

Then you learned something about the earth, I say.

It was hard work, he says. I learned that much.

Are you happy with what you're doing now? I say.

No, he says. I've been doing it too long. The challenge is gone. I've promised myself I'll be out of here by January.

And do what?

That's just it, he says. I'm not sure. Part of me wants to be a singer.

Do it, I say. If you don't, it'll haunt you the rest of your life. Time's just too short not to do what you feel. Look at the world around you. Most people are trapped, doing jobs they can't stand. Before they know it, they've lost the will to break away.

After lunch we go back to the admissions office. Rumors about the man with the pack and the hat with the crow feather have spread. Several of the office workers rush into the lobby to meet me. It's the first realization that I have, concerning how others view me on the trip. I'm someone to be examined and perhaps poked a little to see what I'm made of. I'm a curiosity, a freak, a hero, a sure fire escape or diversion from the day's predictable routine.

I wish I could just take off like you're doing, says Lily, who's in her late twenties and part Cherokee. She's tall and slender and could pass for a dancer. Her eyes are charged with excitement as if she's as hungry as I am to remember just how sweet life can be.

You must be a romantic, I say.

Oh, I am, she says. But I have to watch it. The last guy I got involved with had a good heart, but he was screwed up.

How so? I say.

He worked for a mortician, she says. This old man had died and nobody claimed him. They cremated him and put his ashes in a box. We took him to a bridge and threw him a handful at a time into the river.

That doesn't sound screwed up to me, I say.

No, she says. But that's the part of him I liked. The other part was messed up. He broke into my apartment one night and took everything he could carry. I had no idea he had a coke habit.

I don't find pleasure in her heartache, any more than I did when Hank told me his Chicago-coke-lover story. But hearing their confessions keeps me from feeling like such a fool. Three years ago I fell for an actress in Hollywood who had a nose for the stuff. She stayed straight while I lived in the same town, but when I went back to Alabama, she got addicted to coke again. I swore I'd never see her anymore, and I haven't.

Why don't we cut through the red tape, says Richard, and forget about you staying in the dorm. I've got plenty of room at my place, if you'd like to stay there.

I lift my pack to carry it to Richard's car. I want to see Lily tonight, but I'm shy to ask her with the other office workers breathing down our necks. I make eye contact with her to get at least one more taste.

When are you leaving? she says.

This is encouraging. I can almost smell the back of her neck now. I could offer to phone the funeral home for some ashes. We could go throw them from a bridge in the moonlight.

I have something I want to give you, she says. For the walk. I'll come over to Richard's tonight.

Man, oh, man. My stomach's full, I have a place to stay for the night and a pretty woman's coming over to see me later. Yes, sir, this walking across America could get into a man's blood.

Richard lives only two blocks from the admissions office. He shows me where he hides his extra key and gives me a quick tour of his apartment. When he goes back to his office, I hop into the shower. Hallelujah! The water feels like heaven as it washes away three days of dirt and sweat.

Long after I'm clean I continue to stand beneath the pounding hot water. I soap myself again just to enjoy the sensation of the suds sliding down my body. I've come about fifty-five miles in three days and already my legs are getting harder. I've been wanting to lose about five pounds and half of that is already gone. My stomach is once again taking on that washboard look. I'm disappointed, however, to find that I'm losing some of my hair, caught in the drain.

Why does the air we breathe always seem fresher after we shower? I put on clean clothes and head for downtown Siloam Springs. Without the pack, I'm fifty pounds lighter and, despite sore feet, there's a new bounce in my walk. I'm no longer totally a greenhorn. I've made it into the second state and so far, knock on wood, I'm all in one piece. I am a bit concerned, though, about the weather forecast. Thunderstorms with severe lightning are heading this way.

Downtown is a mile from the college and it looks like a place someone longing for peace and simplicity would dream up. It's only three or four blocks long, with a fire station. A stream twenty feet wide runs through trees and grass while three boys fish. Their red floats ride the ripples while four ducks swim by. One of two dogs barks at the lead duck.

Catching anything? I say.

I almost had one, says the boy in the baseball cap. But he got away.

That wasn't a fish, says the older boy. You were snagged.

I know the difference, says the first boy. I've caught a lot more fish than you have. You even lost that sucker last week. Anybody could catch a sucker.

I can't help it if my line broke, says the older boy. It was *your* pole. Your line was no good.

You jerked too hard, says the other boy, adjusting his baseball cap.

I go on upstream and cross a bridge behind the fire station, where a gazebo sets surrounded by trees. A bench faces the giant creek and a fountain in its center sprays water into the air. An old woman, wearing shades and a red straw hat, throws pieces of bread to the ducks. They quack as they shoot for the treats.

They're hungry, I say.

No, she says. They're not hungry. They just don't have anything better to do. I don't either. My husband died last year. You learn to use your time. My sister likes to quilt and sew. But not me. I don't like being cooped up inside.

She heads on upstream and the ducks follow as she throws pieces of bread. She wads one of the pieces into a tiny ball and tries to hit the biggest bird. She misses and it makes a small splash near the fountain.

You almost got him, I say.

She doesn't hear me or pretends not to. She throws the remaining bread into the creek and disappears behind the fire station. Her tone didn't suggest that she was looking for sympathy, but it reminds me how many lonely old folks there are in America. Back in 1975 I lived with my sister in San Francisco and the lady in the apartment next to us was around eighty. Her name was Billie and she loved to show us old photographs of when she was an actress in Hollywood. She was almost blind and claimed that the bright lights put her eyes out. She lived all alone and never went out. One night she knocked on my door and asked me to rub alcohol on her back.

It's killing me, she said. Won't you please help me?

I went to her place and she lay on her stomach for me to rub her back. I didn't know what to do when she began to moan like a very young woman.

Lower, she said. Just a little lower.

I felt foolish and naive because I hadn't realized till that moment that old people also have physical needs. It was a Friday night and who knows what fantasy stirred within her mind. I rubbed her with the cloth and alcohol a few seconds more. But as her moans got louder I became afraid and left her. It was some time later when I understood that it wasn't sex that she wanted as much as it was that she needed the human touch.

I go back to Richard's apartment at sunset to make sure I don't miss Lily. If I hadn't been so tired when she mentioned coming over I would've thought to set a time. It bugs me to be on the end of a string.

Night falls as I write in my journal. The moon shines down on the cemetery across the street. What a contrast to where I camped under the oak by the Old Baptist Mission Church last night. By now Hank has made it to Texas and learned what's wrong with his mother. I wouldn't want to be in his shoes. If I had his number, I'd call and see how it's going. But maybe it's a good thing I can't reach him. Maybe it's best just to let people come and go. No, that's not right. Not when I'd like to have more friends.

It's going on nine o'clock and Lily still hasn't come. The "older man" within me finds it easy to rationalize that something simply came up for her or she became afraid to expose herself to someone just passing through. No big deal, that's just the way it goes. But to hell with logic, my heart has its side of the story too. She said she was coming and she hasn't even called to offer an excuse. I would've been happy just to have talked awhile. Well, that and maybe held her for a few seconds. I probably could've endured a kiss or two.

I turn on the TV, but I can't escape. I go outside and cross the street into the cemetery. Hundreds of dead stretch below my feet. That I'm alive begins to soothe my frustration.

As my lust and disappointment fade, a lightning bug flashes yellow a few feet away by the tombstone with the carved lamb. I run to catch it, but it's gone. When it flashes again, I grab it and hold it gently in my hand. I cup both hands into a cage and my prisoner lights up a third time, yellowing the finger bars.

I open my hands and the lightning bug crawls up my wrist. It leaps from the hairs on my arm and flashes yellow over the lamb on the tombstone before the darkness swallows it. Isn't it the same with a man's life? A little flicker here, a little flicker there, and then *gulp,* he's swallowed by the earth. Ah, yes, nothing like a cheery bedtime story in the graveyard.

Richard still hasn't returned to his apartment. He's in the chapel with the entire student body. They were required to attend a special meeting where a monk plays a guitar and sings.

I make my bed on the couch and crawl into it. I still wish Lily had come, but I'm over the hurt. Besides, I know that I'm not truly all alone here in the dark. I have the undivided attention of my chiggers, dining as if the night is still young.

The next morning, as I'm leaving town, a car stops with Lily at the wheel. She apologizes for not coming last night and gives me a bag of cookies. As I walk down the Trail I let them melt in my mouth and envision her eyes and more.

# CHAPTER FOURTEEN

T HE MAN WALKING down the road reminds me of Charles Manson. His hair is
wild and curly and he wears no shirt. In his right hand is a rock
big enough to splatter a man's skull from here to New York. His
eyes are crazed, as if the whole world is chasing him and he
wants to say, No more, I'll kill every last one of you. He walks my
way.

I've been on the Trail for almost a week now and my confidence has grown. But I don't relish the thought of having to deal
with a maniac, especially one with a rock in his hand. How does
one greet another walker with murder in his eyes? *Hello, nice day
we're having* just doesn't fill the bill. I could act crazy and howl
before we come within reach of each other. That might give me
the upper hand. It could, however, only serve to make him over-
react and jump me while introducing my head to his trusty rock.

He comes closer with each step and I now see that he has tattoos on both arms. I can't make out what they are, but on his chest is a dragon breathing fire.

If he attacks me, I'm at a great disadvantage with a fifty-pound pack on my back. It could be in my favor if I knocked him to the ground. I could then leap into the air and land atop him to squash him like a TV wrestler. But this isn't TV Land. He might have his own thoughts about just lying there while I execute a Flying Pack.

I don't scare easily, but this is my first experience ever with a crazed man carrying a rock in my direction. Adrenaline shoots through my body and my mind goes weird. What if he's read about me in the newspaper and has fixated on me as some kind of enemy? Maybe he's a white supremacist and hates Indians with all his heart. He could want to knock me off with a rock as some sort of primal ritual.

As he gets to within a few feet of me my instincts take over. I'm ready to slide the pack from me and use it as a shield if I have to. As we step closer toward each other all my senses are heightened. The crunch of his feet against the ground is piercing. The rock in his hand becomes twice as big and the dragon on his chest looks as mean as he does. His eyes are charged with such rage that they seem to bulge from the sockets. His mouth is open and his upper lip is twisted as if he fights for his next breath.

I'm a spring wound too tight. My arms and legs have more energy than they know what to do with. Come on, come on past me, you crazy son-of-a-bitch. Come on by. Come on, *come on.* And finally it's over with. He's behind me and the danger's gone. But *behind* me? I hurry to turn my head and make sure he hasn't lifted the rock. No, he continues on down the road like a man obsessed with purpose and destination.

I've met thousands of people in forty-one years, but most of their faces have become lost in time. I'll *never* forget the caveman who just passed. Who was he and where was he going?

I've been using a map of the Trail of Tears, but I'm not sure which route to take—north or northeast—when I reach Gravette, Arkansas, in the Ozarks. I breeze into the newspaper office and ask the owner if he's up on local history enough to direct me down the Trail.

Not me, he says. You want to talk to Lewis Day. I'll phone him right now and see if he's in.

Lewis Day is in and I'm given directions to the funeral home he owns and operates. I can't say I'm overjoyed about getting a history lesson where a cold body is surrounded by flowers. I must've seen too many Dracula movies when I was a kid. I always have this slight suspicion that a corpse will rise up and grab me.

I take a right two blocks from the newspaper office and see the park with the World War II plane. Across the street from it is the funeral home, and there in the window, with his nose against the glass, is Lewis.

Come right on in, he says. Come right on in and make yourself at home.

I enter his office and the police scanner is on, complete with crackles and pops as a dispatcher gives directions to a car wreck. Why, you old devil you, waiting on a warm one to come in. He appears, however, to be anything but an opportunist: His tone and manners are nothing less than an old-fashioned gentleman. He's seventy-two, and six feet tall with a full head of gray hair. It's easy to imagine him with a mint julep in his hand.

Oh, yes, he says. I know the Trail of Tears in this area like the back of my hand. I've walked twenty-three miles of it myself over the years. Look out the window here. See there, where the ridge starts? That's where the old stagecoach road made the bend and the way the Indians came. My great-grandfather was a full-blooded Cherokee. He lived just down the road here and was a blacksmith for the stagecoach line. Come on outside. I have something to show you.

As we start out the door he cocks an ear to the police scanner. A man can't overlook business too long.

I follow him under a tree and onto the yard to the left of the funeral home. He stops at a rosebush, bursting alive with sixty or seventy red flowers. His eyes beam and his lips part with a smile that can stem only from a great gentle pride.

This bush has been in my family for over 150 years, he says. My Cherokee ancestors brought it from North Carolina in 1830. It's been transplanted four or five times. My parents cared for it while I was in college and in World War II. I'm afraid to move it anymore. Don't think it could take it. I sent a blossom to the National Rose Society. They had never seen one like it before.

It has a great will to live, I say.

I want you to have this, he says.

He reaches down to break a rose from the ancient bush. As he does so his hand trembles and I think of my friend Dan, back in Oklahoma City. He's one of the few men I know who could truly savor this rare moment as the old gentleman hands me the blossom, a trace of his soul.

I'll cherish it all the way back home, I say. I'll include it in the burial ritual I was telling you about.

Do whatever you like, he says. I'm glad you like it. Now, when you go down that hill there, in about, oh, a half mile, you'll come to a spring at the base of a house on your left. That's where the stage stopped. It's also where the Cherokee got water on their march.

We go back to his office. He gives me a detailed map of the Trail on to Missouri. I place the rose in my pack with the buckeye and the apple seeds. I like this old man a lot and shake his hand again just to touch him one more time.

As I go out the door the scanner's volume increases. Business just might be looking up.

I had hoped by now that the days would be cooling off with September winds. But they aren't. The thermometer climbs into the nineties everyday, and now that I'm in the Ozarks the hills are steeper, harder to climb. I've stopped a lot of my bellyaching about the pain in my feet though. I accept it and even look forward to it in a strange kind of way. I want to see if I can handle it and grow from it. It's as if raw determination from my teenage years is being reborn. My body, mind, and spirit are finding a new excitement with each other.

Trees and creeks and birds are no longer *out there*. I'm becoming one with them. In fact, I'm becoming dependent on the loud and jubilant cries of the blue jays. Three or four to a group, they often fly before me and sing as if to promise that all is safe. Some Cherokee believed that they were a sign of good times. When I camp in the evenings, I listen for their calls and pitch my tent under the biggest oak I can find near them. When the darkness quiets them, I depend upon the owl to assure me that I'm in the right spot.

My shirt is soaked with sweat by the time I reach a hilltop overlooking an old house at the next bend. I march to it and find the historic spring, only three or four feet from the road itself. I take off my hat and kneel to the water in the very spot where thousands of Cherokee also did the religious ritual of *going to water*. As if their spirits linger, the water ripples and goosebumps rush up my arms. If the Earth is our Mother, then water must be her heart. How often I have taken it for granted by simply turning a chrome or porcelain handle.

I stick my hands down into the spring and fill them. I raise the cool water to splash my face. I feel I am baptizing myself somehow. I'm washing away old skin, dropping some defenses. As simple—is it simple?—as it is, my life is taking on a new meaning. I have purpose like never before. I'm doing what I believe in, come men with roses or men with rocks. I'm almost in step with my drummer. There's an old Indian saying, *A man's soul can only travel as fast as his feet can carry him.* Perhaps between here and home I'll catch up with myself.

I splash my face again with the spring water, and recall how I loved to draw water from the well at my grandfather's house. Lowering the bucket into the earth and hearing the *splash* when it hit the underground lake seemed like magic. I couldn't wait to crank the windlass to bring the catch to the surface. It was both thrilling and sensual to pull the release trigger and watch the new waterfall rush into the drinking bucket. It was like climbing a tree or swinging on a vine across a creek. A bond was made with Nature, a secret friend who always was there to award me with wonder, to promise me that life would always offer a lift with its mystery. Over the years, living in New Orleans, Chicago, L.A., and San Francisco, I forgot that mystery and failed myself. Some days I could see nothing but work, cars, TV, and people. Nature was nothing more than an old toy. I had buried it without realizing it and didn't know what I longed for when I sometimes ached with loss. I had amputated a part of myself and the phantom lingered. When I would leave the cities and go back to the mountains of Alabama, I would find the power and peace of Nature again. I would swear that I would never again forget it and get caught up in the rat race back in the cities. I didn't lie on purpose.

I lower my hands into the spring again to wash my face and arms. It's cooling as it runs down the skin and I wish that the right woman was here to pour it over my neck and down my back. I would gladly return the favor.

I want to drink from the spring, but I'm afraid to. I can't be sure that it's free of pesticides and bacteria. I walk on.

Back home in Alabama, I've often been amused at how many country drivers wave at total strangers as if they're friends. I have returned their hand-hellos, but never initiated them. I never felt the need. Now, walking down the road, I begin to appreciate that most simple and primitive form of communication. I want to make contact and be part of strangers' lives if only for a fleeting moment. In return for my waves, I get polite waves, surprised waves, gawking waves, amused waves, flattered waves, loving waves, and there are those who refuse to wave but point as if the others in the car are on a tour of roadside attractions. Then there are the guys who nod but don't dare wave because *real men* can't appear too friendly. The truly cool ones simply lift one or two fingers from the steering wheel to let me know they can see me, but don't have time to think about me. Those who hold up their thumbs as if hitchhiking are, I suppose, frustrated artists combing the countryside for the perfect picture to paint.

A truck hauling chickens roars around the coming curve and I grab my hat to prevent it from being blown to the ground. The driver jerks his hand from the stirring wheel and gives me the peace sign. I barely get my hand into the air as he zooms past, to leave a few feathers floating over me and the two horses in the nearby pasture. He isn't the first on the walk to offer the peace sign and I'm amazed each time it happens. I thought the symbol was dead and buried way back yonder in the early seventies. Why, the next thing you know some fool will want to talk about love and understanding.

As I approach Bentonville, Arkansas, the rolling hills stretch before me, covered with small oaks and pastures where horses and cattle graze, goldenrods waving in the breeze along barbed wire fences. A meadowlark sits on a fence post and opens its tiny beak to sing a welcoming song. A creek between two hills meanders into the shaded woods, where an old barn crumbles to the ground, pokeberry bushes hanging heavy with their clusters of purple fruit. A vine snakes around a hickory, and a new squirrel bed rides in the fork of two limbs, the leaves used for the building turning from green to yellow and brown. A hawk circles gently and gracefully overhead as if there's not a worry in the world.

As I get closer to Bentonville, little country houses are re-placed with modern ones. I can't imagine where the money comes from, here in the Ozarks, till I remember that the world's richest man, Sam Walton—owner of Wal-Mart—lives here. Some of his offices and warehouses pad local pockets. Part of me wants to spit anytime I think of a chain store because each one looks just like another one, smothering individuality. But if I spit now, I'll be doing it against the wind. The hat I'm wearing, a gift, came from old Sam's store back in my hometown. I still haven't figured out why they had to chop off the magnificent ridge there to con-struct the building instead of working it into the natural contours of the land. To do such a thing is like taking off a woman's breast when it's in perfect health. I guess they X-rayed and discovered that the earth had a giant tumor or something.

I'm down to my last drop of water and I swear that I'll never take it for granted again as long as I live. I stop at a house with a little office offering tickets to a cave in the backyard. Nobody's here and I bend over a glass case containing arrowheads and human bones found in the cave. When a ghostly shadow falls atop the case, I spin around to find a young man in the doorway.

You work here? I say.

Not usually, he says, but I do today. I'm home for a visit. Ready for it too. I just finished training for Special Forces. The last day we had to walk twenty-six miles with sixty-five pounds on our back. I *ran* the first eight miles. That was a week ago and the feeling hasn't returned to my big toe yet.

As I rolled up my dew-covered tent this morning I promised myself I'd get a motel tonight so I could take a shower. *That won't be necessary,* said my inner voice. *You'll be staying with a family tonight.* Now my head is often juggling thoughts, but when my inner voice speaks I take it as a premonition. Lewis Day was so kind that I just knew he would invite me to stay in his home tonight. Okay, I was wrong about that. But now here's Dough, a fellow walker. That inner voice must've been referring to him and his parents, who own the cave. That, or I was just plain old caught up in wishful thinking when I was half asleep this morning. We go outside and I fill my canteen with water from the garden hose.

In three more days, says Dough, I leave for language school. To study Spanish. Guess I'll be off to Colombia after that to fight in the drug war. Just hope we don't get ourselves into another Vietnam.

Maybe I need to trade my inner voice in on a newer model. Dough doesn't as much as hint that I should spend the night with his folks or even pitch my tent in the yard. I down another mouthful of water and return my canteen to the pack.

Don't forget to duck, I say.

What?

If you go to Colombia, I say.

Oh, yeah, he says. *That* duck.


I arrive in a small Arkansas town, to enter a gas station to use the phone to check on a motel for the night. The cheapest place in town turns out to be Ozark Hill.

Wait a minute, says the mechanic. I heard you on the phone. I got a wife and two kids, but if you don't mind them you can stay at my place tonight. I know what it's like to be on the road. I used to bum around a lot myself.

His name is Bob and he's in his late twenties. He's small and his hands are covered with enough dirt and grease to choke a man who has little will to live. I try to read his eyes to see if I want to accept his invitation. I'm uneasy.

That's a generous offer, I say. You sure your wife won't mind?

No, no, he says. I'm sure. I got another hour to work and she'll be by with the kids to pick us up.

He seems sincere, but I only met the guy five minutes ago. I'm anxious that he has something up his sleeve: A rock, like the man I met on the side of the road? His *voice,* I must hear his voice some more.

I don't want to put you out any, I say.

No, he says. I'm a good judge of character. You'd add something to our evening.

I don't like motels much anyway, I say, offering my hand.

He pulls out a cigarette and lights it. As he blows smoke he looks around us as if to make sure no one can hear us.

I should tell you something right now, he says. Before my wife gets here. It might change your mind.

What are you talking about? I say.

Well, he says. There's something me and my wife like to do at night. We don't let our kids see us, but . . .

Two miles after I passed the man with the rock this morning I saw a paperback book in the weeds alongside the Trail. The title read *Bent Love*. I picked it up and discovered a photograph of two men with a woman. Let's just say she had more than her hands full and appeared to be the happiest person in the world, even if it was a bit painful. I salute the cliche *to each his own,* but if the mechanic is about to suggest a threesome tonight he's barking up the wrong leg.

There's not much I haven't seen, I say. Why don't you just spit it out?

He takes another draw from the cigarette, blows a cloud of smoke, and drops it to the ground. He crushes the cigarette with his foot.

Like I said, he says, we don't let our kids see us and we only do it at night. What I'm trying to say is that we like to smoke a little dope to unwind. Do you smoke or will it bother you when we do?

Welcome to America: Down the road I met a soldier in the drug war and now I meet a rebel in the counterforces. No doubt about it, our streets aren't lined with gold, they're lined with dope.

I don't smoke, I say. What you and your wife do is your business.

You didn't strike me as somebody who'd play God, he says. Just thought I'd check it out before it was too late. A lot of people confuse grass with crack or smack. We don't do any hard drugs, but I have to have a little something at night to deal with this shit job. It's all I can do to make ends meet one week to the next. I got a dream to help keep me going though. Come back here and I'll show you.

# CHAPTER FIFTEEN

H E LEADS ME into the garage, where a car motor sets on an iron stand. He eyes it much like Lewis Day did his rosebush.

I built it myself, says Bob. It's for a dragster I'll take to the Tulsa Racetrack. One more month and she'll be ready to burn rubber. My wife doesn't like me doing this though. I have to work extra hours to pay for parts.

I love to hear people get excited about their dreams. It's as though their energy comes into my body to feed me and further awaken my own hopes. I feel sad for those who never dream, not only because they're in pain but because it makes me hesitant to release my own enthusiasm. For many years I didn't realize why I was uncomfortable around those who have never hungered to turn the bend or explore a new thought. I wondered if I was a freak. Even today, when I meet people who don't get excited about being alive I have to remind myself to have compassion instead of disgust. Sometimes I fail and just don't give a damn. I get far away from those people as quickly as I can. I'm not proud of sometimes being selfish.

Did you learn to work on cars, I say, when you were a kid?

Yeah, he says, I've loved to work with tools as long as I can remember. It's like I can put my mind in order with my hands. Keeps me out of trouble too. See this scar on the back of my arm? That's where an inmate stabbed me with a fork. Several years back I did fifteen months for operating a chop shop. I could blowtorch a hot car in nothing flat. Anyway, I was in the chow line when the guy behind me accused me of getting in front of him. Man, you talk about hurting. When he stuck that fork in my arm, he twisted it like I was a plate of spaghetti. You can figure out what the sauce was.

I ease my fingers over the motor, his dream machine.

Every part of this motor, says Bob, has been balanced as fine as the guts of a Swiss watch.

I can see you coming across the finish line right now, I say. The other cars are eating your smoke.

That's right, he says. That's exactly right. Yeah, eating my smoke—*zoom!*

While we wait on Bob's wife and kids to arrive, he lights a blowtorch to cut iron bars. He welds them together to make truck beds. Judging by the expression on his face, it's about as much fun as digging a ditch or picking a field of cotton with two sore hands. Still, I'm intrigued with a fire hot enough to blaze through iron. When the molten piece comes apart, his tired eyes flicker with victory.

Bob's wife, Sallie, arrives in a Mustang with their two children. She's freckled with red hair and makes me think of pictures I've seen of those who moved from Oklahoma to California during the dust bowl days. Bob breaks the news to her about me staying with them tonight, and it seems to make her about as happy as getting a briar in her finger.

Okay, she says. Let's just get home. I'm tired.

I'm tempted to jump ship and head on to the motel. But when I see the kids, Danny, five, and Brenda, three, I can't resist: Their tender eyes, beaming with curiosity, nail me. A part of me is as young as them and I can't wait to play. Who are those two big people in the front seat anyway? Why are they saying the strange things they're saying?

Are you listening? says Bob, starting the car.

I *heard* you, says Sallie. I don't think it's a good idea to change jobs right now.

But Bill's sure he'll do enough business, says Bob, to hire me full-time. I can just work on motors. No more welding.

And what happens if his new garage, says Sallie, doesn't go over? You'll be out of a job.

Me and the other two kids in the backseat don't have to use words to talk. Our eyes are somehow connected and plugged into this gigantic amusement park: This car, this road, those trees and horses, us—everything is just a little bit funny.

I can wiggle my ears, says Danny. See? I can do it better in the morning after I've slept.

Brenda laughs and her mother turns around to eye us. In a single flash I see a whole new side. She smiles as if I've passed an important test with her children and she wants to apologize for any toes she stepped on when we met.

Five miles later we arrive at an old farmhouse surrounded by oaks. Night is falling and Bob, still covered with grease and dirt, insists that I take a bath before him. I feel a little foolish that I didn't trust him at first. I'm not sure why I always get just a bit choked up when strangers let me into their lives as if I were a long-lost friend. I don't usually think of myself as a desperate human being.

The smell of hamburger steaks and french fries drifts into the bathroom as Sallie cooks in the adjoining room. There's no shower and the tub doesn't have a regular stopper. I like using the sock she gave me because it reminds me I'm in a home free of pretense.

I can't remember the last time I soaked in a tub and I stretch out all the way to paradise. I close my eyes and float in the Fountain of Youth. I have reached Soul Harbor. I don't have a worry in the world and life, it seems at the moment, is not only rich but eternal. As they used to say back in the sixties, what a trip.

Sallie has prepared a salad with the hamburger steaks and french fries and I go back for seconds. I walked twenty-three miles today and as many calories as I'm burning I can eat to my heart's content without fear of gaining an ounce. I've already lost the five pounds I wanted to leave on someone's doorstep. I weigh 170 pounds, but if my metabolism doesn't adjust to the walk I'll be skin and bones by the time I reach home. *Home,* God, it seems a million miles from here. But I can't think in those terms. I have to live one day at a time. One step after the other.

Danny tries to twirl his plastic ray gun and demonstrate karate kicks at the same time. My new job is to watch as if my life depends on it.

I suggest we team up, I say. You go with me on this walk and we'll clean up America.

I don't think Mother'll let me, he says. How about when I'm older? You want to borrow my ray gun?

Brenda demands equal time by placing her cat, Blue, in my

lap. In her other hand she carries a stuffed Garfield, who's also just dying to meet me. I hate to blow my own horn, but I'm rather proud of eating with two cats in my lap while scoring karate kicks at the same time.

Did you see that one? says Danny. Did you see how high it was?

That was a good meal, if I say so myself, says Sallie. Oh, and what a day. I go to college, but I work part-time at a pawn shop too. I don't like it. You see people when they're scraping bottom. Like this afternoon, this woman comes in with a gold watch. At least, she thought it was gold. I couldn't give her much for it and she thought I was just being mean. I don't like to see people hurting. Especially when they blame me. That a blister you're fooling with? Here, I'll get you a safety pin.

She goes after the pin and I'm thinking again how lucky I am to have met this family. But a knock at the door puts a kink in the night.

I wonder who that is? says Bob, rising from his chair.

Sallie returns with the pin as Bob opens the door. A tall man about my age enters with a human skull in his hands. He hides the skull as best he can as Danny and Brenda give him the eye. Bob introduces him as Fred and leads him into the kitchen.

I thought I had kicked the picture of the man with the rock, but I was wrong. As soon as I saw the skull I was back on the Trail again with the crazed eyes coming toward me.

My heart begins to beat faster and this is no longer home sweet home. I wish I were in the woods inside my tent with only an owl and the wind for friends.

I stick the pin into the blister on my foot and water runs from it. Danny and Brenda soon fall asleep and Bob carries them to the water bed in the next room. Fred comes from the kitchen with the skull as if he's Hamlet ready to speak of Death.

The skull, a porcelain pipe for smoking grass, is lighted and I hide inside my journal. It's not that I'm a stranger to weed or other mind-altering chemicals. I grew up in the sixties and did my share of flips and turns off the high board. But since the romantic days of *Easy Rider* I've met a lot of people with problems who smoke dope. I turn my back on it and write in my journal.

You got pads in your shoes? says Fred.

The skull has been put away and I'm calm again. Sallie and I are watching TV while Fred and Bob play chess.

No, I say, massaging my feet.

I put some in my boots, he says. I'm a machinist and on my feet all day. The pads help, but my boots aren't really big enough. It's not much, but I'd be happy if you'd take 'em as a contribution to your walk. I've always felt that Indians got the short end of the stick.

He takes off his cowboy boots and hands me the pads. They're too big and Sallie gets a pair of scissors so I can cut them down. As I slide the pads into my Reeboks, Fred moves his knight to protect his queen. In less than an hour he has gone from a stranger with a skull coming from the night to a gentle and generous soul with a kingdom at his fingertips. Ah, if only all men could transform themselves so quickly, or if I could only see into their hearts with more clarity.

Damn it, says Bob. I didn't think you could beat me. Want to go again?

On the couch, I awake in the middle of the night. Tree limbs scratch against the roof as the wind stirs and I get up to go to the bathroom. To get there I must pass by the waterbed where Bob,

Sallie, Danny, and Brenda all float in sleep. I can't afford to stop and study them. If Bob awoke he might misread why I'm so intrigued. It's simple: I savor the bond between parents and children that I don't have. This isn't envy. I value my freedom more than love. So I tell myself anyway.

I go back to the living room and cover myself on the couch. It's warm and cozy here and it feels good to know that Danny and Brenda are safe and well at home with their parents. A cricket chirps in the darkness between me and the family floating on the water bed. Its song is so loud that it seems to bounce off the walls and echo throughout the old country house. This is undoubtedly an Olympic cricket, for thirty minutes later its legs are still going strong. Its song, however, has dropped from the charts as far as I'm concerned. Each chirp takes a bite out of my sleep.

Shh, whispers Sallie. Shut up. Did you hear me? I said *shut up*.

Thank God, Sallie hears it too. I was beginning to think I'd have to go nuts alone in the dark. Don't get me wrong, one of my best friends was a cricket. Remember Walt Disney's Jiminy Cricket? I can still see him on TV, hopping from book to book in the library as he sings *I'm no fool, no, sir-ree, I want to live to be one hundred and three* . . .

The next morning it's raining like hell. Thunder sounds in the near distance and I'm afraid I'll be struck by lightning when I start walking. Bob and Sallie invite me to stay another night, but the road calls.

I have a raincoat, I say. But do you have a plastic bag to cover my hat?

This is all I can find, says Sallie, coming from the kitchen.

She hands me a plastic bag and it fits my hat like a glove. Written across the center is Kentucky Fried Chicken. Just call me colonel for short.

As we ride to the station where Bob works, the rain pounds the car. I'm a bit tempted to kick myself in the ass for not accepting their invitation to stay another night. It's not as if I have a meeting on Madison Avenue.

Remember what I said? says Danny. Remember, I said I could do it better in the morning? See, look at my ears.

His ears wiggle as if he were the finalist in a national Ear-wiggling Contest, and damned if I couldn't hug him right now for pulling me out of my slump over the rain. I try to wiggle my ears too. Danny isn't exactly swept off his feet.

Try your nose, he says. It's a little easier for some people.

Bob and I get out at the station, and it hurts to watch Sallie drive away with Danny and Brenda because I may never see them again. I can't help but wonder if I haven't been playing a game for many years to see just how many memories I can pack into my mind and heart.

See you at the racetrack, I say, slipping into my raincoat.

Yeah, says Bob, doing as poor a job as me in hiding his feelings. See you at the finish line.

I walk into the rain and hit the Trail again. I pray that the thunder and lightning keep their distance. The pads Fred gave me soften my steps as my shoes become soaked. To passing motorists I must look like a homeless man trying to sell Kentucky Fried Chicken. From time to time, I try to wiggle my ears.

# CHAPTER SIXTEEN

TWO DAYS LATER it's still raining, but the thunder and lightning are kind to stay away. In the distance, however, I see the giant flickers and hear the booms as if a war builds.

In Pea Ridge National Military Park the Trail takes me across the battlefield where Yanks and Rebs alike got their eyeballs shot out or their legs sawed off by doctors, with only whiskey to deaden the pain. My great-grandfather fought in the Civil War; I find myself starting to whistle, *When Johnny comes marching home again, hurrah, hurrah. When Johnny comes marching home again, hurrah, hurrah.*

This is also the battlefield where the Cherokee Chief Stand Watie led one thousand Cherokee braves against the Union. On horses, they fought with bows and arrows and could get off two or three shots before the soldiers could reload their guns. Watie was the last general to surrender when the Civil War ended, because he didn't know that Lee had thrown in the towel.

As I walk from the battlefield, I approach an old house that is little more than a shack with another wooden and weathered building next to it. They look as though a strong wind could turn them into firewood. On a post is a sign, painted as if by a child, with the words:

WHITE OAK

HANDMADE BASKETS

FOR SALE

I step onto the wooden porch and take the pack from my back. The rain on the tin roof creates a soothing and needed song after walking where so many men were killed. I can't help but think that whoever lives here is someone I met before. I knock and footsteps soon come my way. The door opens and an old Indian eyes me as if I have come at a bad time.

You the one who makes the baskets? I say.

He leads me into the next building, which is filled with baskets of all shapes and sizes. Except for a light bulb dangling overhead, the room could be 150 years old. I pick up one basket after another and examine them. I don't know what I'm looking for. They just feel good to my touch. I imagine them filled with blackberries, strawberries, squash, tomatoes, and corn. But I also hear the oak from which they're made crashing to the ground. The wrinkled Indian doesn't look Cherokee and I can't place his tribe. He stands by the door where the rain falls and watches me with guarded eyes.

You want to buy one? he says.

I explain that I'm walking to Alabama and that I don't have room for a basket. I ask his tribe. He answers Apache, but doesn't offer another word. I can't decide if he doesn't trust me or if I simply have to build a bridge between us.

You remind me of my grandfather, I say. He worked with his hands all his life. He was the last man in my county to go to town in a buggy. He had the last water-driven gristmill in the area. I think older people are more interesting than those my age. They're more sure of themselves and are more at peace.

How old do you think I am? he says.

Sixty-five?

I'm eighty-eight, he says.

You look in great health, I say. You must enjoy life.

I exist, he says. That's all. I exist.

If you could change anything in America, I say, what would you change?

I'm a radical, he says, his voice rising. I'd change the laws about old people. See to it that they got more money and better care. I'd get rid of all our congressman and start over with new ones.

Yep, that did it. Now that Mr. Ben Conway has tapped into his passion and gotten a thorn or two out of his chest he's ready to be friendly. He takes me into a third shack, his workshop, and shows me how he uses a special plane to cut thin strips of white oak to weave his baskets just like his grandfather taught him in Arizona.

I can teach a man how to make 'em in just one week, says Ben, if he'll *listen*. Don't many folks know that art. It's about as rare as weaving baskets from oak these days. I want you to meet my wife, he continues, but you stay out here while I ask her if she's up for company. She's been a little down lately. Trouble with her hip.

He hurries into the house and returns a few seconds later. He tells me that his wife, Mary, says to come on in. I can't believe that she's ninety-one. She sits on a hot water bottle to comfort her hip, but she has more energy and curiosity than women I've met who were twenty-five. She insists on making us coffee to have with a tin box filled with Oreos.

Indians didn't used to cry, she says. Did you know that? Well, they didn't. The white man taught 'em how to cry. They pushed 'em and kicked 'em till they had to learn tears.

I built this house myself, says Ben, biting into another cookie. Built it back in 1947. Want me to heat that water bottle, honey?

No, she says. I'm fine. Now, you're a guest. You take another one of those cookies or you'll hurt my feelings.

I built the workshop too, says Ben. Did you see my three cars? They're worth fifteen hundred dollars. Mary makes money selling dolls. Tell him what you do.

Oh, she says, it ain't much. I've made a few apple dolls in my time. You cut the apple into a head and dry it out. It's a lot of work, but they're real cute. I once made a Penny Doll and sent it all the way to England to Queen Elizabeth. You've seen 'em. Made out of wood with movable legs and arms. The queen herself sent me a thank-you note. Now, go ahead and do like I said. Get another one of those cookies. You got to have your energy to walk.

Mary was married to a Cherokee before she met Ben. They had a son, but he died; her husband followed. She and Ben don't have any kids.

Do you wish you did have children? I say as I reach for another cookie.

No, says Ben. Not with the way the world is today. There's too much greed and violence. Money, money, money . . . No, man is out of step with where he came from. That water bottle need heating up?

Ben once created saddles and carved them with fancy designs just like he did the holsters he made. All four walls are covered with over one hundred silver and rusty horse bits. It's as if Ben has placed them there to stay in the middle of a great, wild, and eternal herd. As I watch him chew his Oreo I'm struck with a sadness I don't want. I wonder what will become of him when Mary dies. Then the biting truth sets in: I'm not so worried about them as I am about myself when I get old and sit alone. Perhaps I'll nibble a cookie and recall this moment as crumbs fall to the floor.

The coffee break is over. I take one more Oreo and hit the Trail to eat it as I walk. It's still raining, but I'm determined to make it to the Missouri line by dark.

As night approaches, the wind begins to gust and I grab a burger and fries in a little joint only minutes before it closes. It looks like the rain could become a storm any minute and the nearest motel is twenty miles away. I'm tempted to explain my situation to the waitress and see if I can go home with her. But I don't. I fish some money from my pocket for the check and hurry out the door. I've got to find a place to pitch my tent before darkness swallows me.

The wind is getting stronger by the minute. Lightning and thunder are coming closer. It's almost dark when, a couple of miles up the road, I enter a ghost town. Several stone and wooden buildings are falling apart. A woman in a yellow raincoat appears between two of them but disappears into the twilight as if she knows a secret opening. I'm not truly afraid nor do I really feel safe. Let's just call it a first-degree burn of anxiety.

A board dangles from an old feed mill and a piece of the tin roof rattles near where the woman first appeared. I get the shit scared out of me when something like a giant white jellyfish shoots across the road in front of me to lift ten feet up into the air and crash against the feed mill. I'm relieved to discover that it's only a sheet of plastic.

I consider taking shelter in the feed mill, but decide to pitch my tent between stone buildings farther up the road. If the light rain does become a storm, I'll at least be somewhat protected from the wind.

The ground doesn't care for my plan. It's so damn hard that my tent's stakes, made from coat hangers, bend into zigzagged sculptures. I finally get them a couple of inches into the soil. I cross my fingers that they won't jerk loose in the night to leave me tangled in a nylon web.

Tent Hotel won't make it as a new chain across America. But I'm dry here and I have my pocket radio to help me fight the Rainy Night Blues. It pops and crackles with lightning as a Tulsa station tries to come through with the last thing I want to hear: Thunderstorms are forecast throughout the night and tomorrow, *severe at times.* I change stations and get Bob Dylan, singing "Lay, Lady, Lay." It's the song I lived by when I did the weekend hitchhiking marathons from the University of Alabama to Oklahoma City to see Carole, my ex-wife. I wouldn't mention her again, but here's this song and I've dreamed of her twice already since I left Tahlequah. The karma gods must be having a blast watching me. It's not enough I had to thumb from Alabama to Oklahoma and back many times. Now I've got to walk it. Whatever I did in my previous life, if I had one, apparently fell just a little short of a standing ovation. Just listen to me, getting shook up over the weather forecast and trying to hold something besides myself responsible for being here.

Throughout the night the tin roof rattles in the wind and a steady rain falls. It's hard to sleep and when I do, I awake with my hand pressed so hard against the ground that water seeps into the tent. It's as though the weather wants to make it extra clear that I'm fair game.

I had trouble sleeping one rainy night like this when I was a child. My uncle told me that an Indian, no taller than a rabbit, lived behind a big rock at the little waterfall in the creek behind his barn. I was afraid that the rain would wash him away and I'd never see him. Every time I went to my uncle's house during this period I ran to the creek as soon as I arrived. I thought I found the little Indian's footprints in the mud, but he would never let me see him and I couldn't understand why.

The Little People, according to the Cherokee, were Indians between one and three feet tall. They lived in the woods or behind waterfalls or in the sagebrush fields. Just put out some bread or beans for them by the trees and they'll eat it in the night. If an acorn drops on your head, be quick to eye the oak, for Little People could be in the limbs playing with you. They, too, are Cherokee and like to roll down hills and laugh. If you *do* see one, don't brag about it. Keep it close to your heart and you will stay warm inside. If you are lonely or in need, they will help you. Don't cry when your mother dies, for the Little People will take her by the hand and lead her to the Great Spirit.

I awake at dawn with the wind going crazy, as lightning and thunder orchestrate a blasting downpour. I get dressed and crawl from the tent to pull the stakes from the mud. I'm not as discouraged as I am plain old pissed off. There's nowhere to have breakfast or even a cup of coffee. A truly wise man might simply tell himself to go with the flow. Whether I want to do that or not, I may soon have no choice. Rain is falling with such intensity that it's filling the ditches along the road and washing over my feet.

I'm a man in a tub of water with a naked wire on a thread dangling from the ceiling. At least, that's how I feel.

If I'd had any common sense I would've found shelter in the feed mill or another one of the ghost buildings where I camped last night. But, no, not me. I had to start walking at dawn as if my life depended on it. Surely to God I don't have a death wish.

For two hours now I'm walking in this storm. For a mile or so the thunder and lightning turn my stomach inside out. Then the rain will let up and I can almost taste a clear sky. *Boom!* The whole explosion starts again and I'm sure this is the last mile I'll ever walk. I see someone finding me dead on the side of the road with my face in the mud. My hat, still sporting the plastic Kentucky Fried Chicken bag, floats down a ditch. My ID is checked and the police phone my parents.

I wanted him to get a regular job, says my father.

It's all *my* fault, says my mother.

Three drivers have stopped to offer me rides and the second one swore that I should skip the next town, five miles up the road, because folks there look for trouble. *Low-down trouble.* Great, just what I need.

They say truth can overtake a man when he least expects it. This is true for me right now, because just as I think I'm about to break, when lightning flashes almost close enough to singe my hair, I'm forced to really look at myself. All my life I've finished *second* or *third.* Not bad, not bad at all. But, still, just another *also-ran.* Here, now—regardless of what others think—I have a chance to be the *first* man to walk the Trail of Tears since the Cherokee. I may not do it with the greatest grace in the world, but I've got to do it. I've got to do it even if it means I may die. There, now I've said it. It's out in the open. This doesn't make the fear go away. But it gives me added strength to go on. Like the lightning I, too, have a power. I have the power of choice to be here or not and I understand for the first time what my friend, Paul, in New York meant about the ultimate choice: We had gone to a bar in the East Village one night and he confessed that twenty years ago, while in the French Foreign Legion, he had killed many men in Africa.

I'm not proud of this, he had said. But I'm fighting with it again. I'm fighting the urge to kill somebody because of the feeling. It gives me true *power*. Don't you see? The ultimate choice, the greatest high, is to realize just how precious and vulnerable life is from breath to breath. Of course, the healthy thing is to feel that power without hurting anyone. To do so, you must risk your life at something you believe in. You've never killed another human being. I wish I were that lucky, but when you're twenty years old what do you really know about life?

If I'm a madman, so be it. But when lightning flashes again, I tell myself there is such a force as destiny. It's not my time to go. Not now that I'm entering middle age and starting to make heads and tails of things. I have made the right choice and I will be rewarded for it with safety. Still, my steps quicken as thunder crashes.

Despite having seen enough rain the past few hours to float a battleship, I rejoice on spotting a water tower. On it is written WASHBURN, the forewarned low-down trouble town. But saying it's a town is stretching it a bit. A crossroads with a grocery store is more like it. The rain has let up and the thunder and lightning have, at last, stopped—hallelujah. People all along the Trail have been too warm and kind for me to believe that folks here will be any different. Hey, it just now strikes me that *I'm in Missouri.* I'm in my *third* state in one week. Yes, indeed, Boss, bronze those blisters.

Soaked to the bone, I enter the general store without a trace of doubt that I'll be received like a half-drowned man grateful to be alive. Boy, am I off target. The store is packed with men eating at booths and playing pool as if to do anything else would be a disgrace to their calling in life. Me? Well, judging by how they size me up and down, I'm a wet rat who'd better not leave any tracks on the floor. Hey, I think, I'm a man with power. I've just walked on lightning. You can't mess with me. I'll win you over.

Hello, I say, as if making a rather concise speech.

*Crash* go the pool balls. The good old boys eye me closer yet. The one with the wooden match, working it from side to side in his mouth, offers a grin which I feel could cut glass faster than a diamond. Now, I grew up in Alabama, which as everybody knows is the Redneck Capital of the world. I've chewed the fat with good old boys who fight roosters and bulldogs just because they're there. But these fellers here in this store frankly give me the damn jitters.

I order a tuna sandwich and a cup of coffee and go outside to eat by my lonesome. Actually, I really don't give a shit that they're not more friendly in there.

I'm so thankful that the storm let up that I'm happy just to know I made it to Missouri. I eat the tuna sandwich, take a couple sips of the coffee, and take off again on my merry way toward Springfield. This is an important town on the trip because once I land there I can cut east—toward home. Then, too, since I wasn't received in the store like anything more than a rat washed up on the shore, I celebrate my loneness. I have walked on fire and lived to recall it. Or like a snake in the night, is that force in Nature simply coiling into another form to grab me by the balls and jerk, when I least expect it?

Whatever, I whistle as I head on up the winding road. The sun is trying its best to shine through, when I spot a sign saying O'VALLON WINERY. Oh, yes, friends and neighbors, I could use a

taste of Bacchus right about now. I don't care what kind of a
realization occurs, lightning definitely dries out a man's mouth.

Another half mile up the Trail I spot a beautiful old farmhouse, converted into a winery. I can't brag that I approach it
with a delicate walk. I'm more like a camel in the desert whose
hump is empty, when he discovers a palm towering over a bubbling spring.

It's not so much that I want to get loaded, as I savor a dry
place to sit and relax. Only one car is parked outside the winery
and I'm concerned that it may be closed. But when I turn the
doorknob, the door opens to a man in his fifties who wears a
grin.

Come in, he says. Come in.

I'm pretty wet, I say.

Well, he adds, you've picked a good place to dry off. Like a
cup of coffee?

I was thinking of wine, I say.

Wine, he says. Oh, yes, wine. That's what we make here. I
might even join you for a taste or two.

Frank England, a retired veterinarian, inherited this farm
from his grandfather. He converted it into a winery five years ago.
Last year his spirits won six medals. He pours two whites to start
and I don't have the slightest trouble in getting them to go down.
Ah, yes, it's so easy to imagine yourself an adventurer when
you're in a room stacked with bottles of inspiration.

Like to taste the reds now? says Frank.

I feel obligated, I say, to honor your hard work.

Yes, says Frank, I'm glad you reminded me of that. I'll have
to join you with the reds as well.

For the next hour we sit sipping the stuff poets are made of,
and I find Frank to be the perfect host after my less-than-wel-
come dip into the Washburn general store. Between tastes, he

takes me out back to see giant stainless-steel vats being pumped
full of juice from grapes, their hulls creating a mound three feet
high.

See over there? he says. That's where Herman Jaeger saved a
whole vineyard from disease by grafting another grapevine onto
it. Over one million acres have been done the same way in
France. Right here, in this very spot, is where George Washington
Carver worked for him one summer. It won't make the history
books, but it's also famous for me because it's where I played
with a traveling band of Gypsies when I was six years old. And
back on that battlefield in Pea Ridge where Stand Watie and his
Cherokee filled the Union soldiers full of arrows? My grandfather
was eight at the time and saw it all. After the battle, he sneaked
onto the field and dragged a saddle home.

We go back into the winery and I decide that I've bummed
enough wine for one day. But I'm not ready to push on, so I buy a
bottle of the white and open it. I pour a glass as Frank handles a
phone call. I've only had a total of two glasses, but that's enough
to make me feel the magic of the walk. *Magic?* Did someone say
*magic*? Yes, remember when we were children and every day was
a new adventure filled with wonder and suspense? We had no
bills, no job, no obligation but to look and listen to the fantastic
show all around us. Yes, that is what I feel right now. I am a child
on the Trail of Tears. Time has no beginning. Time has no end.
Anything is possible.

You leaving already? says Frank. I haven't told you my jokes.
Did you know you can judge a wine buyer by the car he drives? A
man in a *new* Cadillac buys one bottle. A man in an *old* Cadillac
buys three bottles. A man in a Winnebago buys a bottle of the
sweetest wine you have and returns the next year to buy another
bottle because the first one's almost gone. It's the man in a Volks-
wagen who buys a case.

* * *

I head on up the road and the sun sets as three blue jays squawk like crazy to fly into a grove of massive and towering oaks. I take it as a good omen and march into the woods to camp for the night. I set up my tent on a bed of soft leaves and finally manage to build a fire from the damp limbs of a fallen tree.

Long ago, *very* long ago, when the Earth was cold, the Thunders sent a bolt of lightning to create *fire* in a sycamore tree, growing on an island. Many creatures dared to cross the water to get the fire, but they failed. It was the delicate and silent water spider who spun a tusti bowl and placed it on her back that finally made it to the island to bring back a tiny glowing coal.

I take the white wine from my pack and drink right from the bottle as I sit with my back against an oak. The fire casts a spell; I feel I could be living over a thousand years ago as twilight settles over me and the leaves, the smell of the moist earth rising to my nose like a promise of greater mystery yet to come.

I'm placing a new branch onto the fire when it appears over the treetops like a creature from my innermost dreams. In the shape of a cross, a giant crane glides over and I begin to chant as I stand and dance. It, of all birds, is the one I consider my guide on the walk. It is almost always alone and flies with a great sense of grace. The Cherokee considered it a very spiritual bird and from it I believe I draw great strength as I chant and dance to watch it fade into the twilight.

It vanishes, but the chanting and dancing must continue. It's the first crane I've seen on the journey and I believe it has presented itself to reward me for making it through the storm. As I chant I feel I connect with its spirit and those who passed this way in 1838 on the Trail of Tears. But it's not enough for me to chant and dance around the fire. I remove my shoes so I can touch the earth and know her power as well.

I'm still dancing and chanting as the moon appears. Who can prove God doesn't shine on me at this very moment, the fire crackling and popping like a magic ball of light rising from the soil? Yes, Master—in whatever form or shape You truly take—I'm here to celebrate my flesh and soul.

That night, inside the tent, I watch the glowing embers fade into the night. I don't fully understand it, but I have, as of today, shed an important layer of skin. The walk is changing me, transforming me into—what? I fall asleep and awake to an owl hooting in an oak over me. The fire is gone except for a faint glow beneath the ashes. The moon shines down on my tent and here, lying on a bed of leaves, I realize I have stored bolts of lightning in my body with the flight of a crane. At least one foot has entered the Spirit World. Now anything is truly possible. I wrap my arm around my pack and snuggle up for sleep and await the mystery of another day.

I awake again. This time from a dream: I hold a baby in my arms. It is a baby that came from my insides. I'm as happy as a lark.

The morning is, for the first time, crisp with autumn. A cool breeze plays in the leaves as I roll my tent and stuff it in the pack. The fire is now no more than ashes and my dancing footprints are faint in the earth. My baby is gone and I am left alone again with my crow feather and snake rattler. But I feel full and begin walking beneath a sky free of rain, thunder, and lightning. Somewhere in the area a crane also begins a new day.

# CHAPTER SEVENTEEN

M ARY'S CAFÉ LOOKS inviting, so I enter to have breakfast. I'm intrigued to find the walls alive with framed arrowheads and prints of Indian Chiefs. When the waitress discovers what I'm up to, she invites me back to meet her sister, Linda, who is part Cherokee and owns the café. She's so excited about the walk that I'm invited to sit at the family table.

Breakfast is on the house, she says. I want you to take something with you for the burial ritual too.

She digs into her purse.

Do you realize you're looking at a dead person? she says. The doctors gave me two weeks to live a few years back. I had cancer of the gut. I almost did die too. After my operation, I left this world. I was walking down this dark green path when I saw the lips of Jesus. He told me it wasn't my time to go and I turned back. I took painful treatments for fifteen months. Anyway, here it is, she adds, pulling a two-inch silver cross from her purse. I've had it for fifteen years. It helped me get through the cancer. Maybe it'll help you on the walk.

I usually get uncomfortable when someone mentions Jesus, as Linda did on giving me the cross, because I'm leery that a speech is coming about God and morals and all that. But this isn't the case here. She simply wants to give part of her heart to what I'm doing. I'm seeing this in people every day on the walk, whether they give me things or simply their interest and best wishes. Far more than I had imagined before I began the journey, it is touching a chord deep inside the human spirit. I question if I'm truly worthy of all the kindness. Linda phones a friend at the local newspaper who's also part Cherokee. She comes to the café to interview me and goes home to return with an arrowhead for me. Is it possible that the Indian who made the relic, hundreds of years ago, could have dreamed how his work would live on? We're all only fragile threads, but what a tapestry we make.

Evangel College in Springfield lets me have a dorm room for two nights. At last, I can do my laundry.

In the dorm lobby, watching *Star Trek* on TV, I come to a decision. I've wanted the walk to be pure and as spiritual as possible. But the reality is that the Trail wanders through a modern America which is as tainted as me. Also, I'm meeting people who've never heard of the Trail of Tears and I want the country to be informed. I decide to contact the Springfield TV stations about my walk.

Rested, I pack my clean clothes and head east for five miles down Route 60 to a store where I await a TV reporter to interview me. The cashier, overhearing my story, phones her mother. She comes with a most peculiar piece of jewelry.

My ancestors made the walk in 1838, says Shirley Rice. This necklace has been passed on from generation to generation. The black seeds represent the children who died. The gold balls are the old people who passed on. I can't give it to my daughter when I go, because she doesn't have enough Indian blood. Each time my ancestors have died, a gold ball has been taken from the strand and buried with them. When I die, the necklace will be buried with me over my left ear.

She opens a black box the size of her hand. She removes a dime from a bed of cotton and hands it to me.

This has been kept with the necklace, she says, since 1943 in a trunk in the attic. I want you to take it back to the old homeland in Alabama. Bury it with your other gifts.

I hope to find a television in a store or café so I can see myself on the six o'clock news. But I'm in the middle of nowhere when the time rolls around. I liked the reporter who interviewed me. He was warm and easy to talk to, but I can't be sure how he edited the tape. It dawns upon me with greater clarity just what a responsibility I've taken on to speak to millions about why I'm out here walking. What if I look like a fool, or worse yet, what if some nut or white supremacist is upset by the story and decides that I'll look better with a bullet in my head? Great, just the thought I need running through my mind as the sun sets and I haven't found a place to camp.

I push on for an hour after dark and finally find a lone oak near the Trail. I pitch my tent by the light of the moon and crawl into my nylon womb while a coyote howls in the distance. An owl hoots in my dreams and I can't prove that it's not a lonely Cherokee man.

The old Indian warned her daughter that she must marry a man who was a good hunter. A man finally appeared one day to make such a claim. He wasn't so good-looking, but the old mother encouraged the daughter to accept his proposal. They were married and the first day he went out to hunt he returned with only three small fish. He promised that he'd do better the next day, but he brought in only two skinny spring lizards. The third day produced only bits of deer meat left behind by more fortunate hunters. The daughter was uneasy about her new husband and the old mother whispered that she should follow the man and see just what his problem was. The next day the man went into the woods to fish and the daughter tiptoed behind him. When he came to the river he changed into a hooting owl and flew down to grab a small crawfish from the sand. As he turned back into a man his wife ran back home through the woods. He arrived a couple of minutes later with the crawfish.

This is all you caught? she said.

An owl frightened all the fish away, said the man.

*You* are the owl, said the woman. I need a man.

She packed his bag and drove the owl into the woods. He sat in a tree to forever feel his grief of lost love as he hooted in the night.

The next day drivers honk and wave as if they know me. The amount of peace signs being thrown my way has tripled. When a new Cadillac stops up ahead of me, I'm not sure what to think. It's parked right in my path and I approach it with caution. The driver, a big man with a beard, rolls down his window.

I saw you on TV last night, he says. Glad to see somebody doing something besides sitting on his ass.

I do my share of that too, I say. One of my favorite hobbies.

America's going to hell, he says. We need more people doing what they believe in. Everybody thinks the other guy should do it. I respect a man who isn't afraid to take a chance. I'm a construction man myself, but on the weekends I sing Gospel songs with my family. Didn't used to though. All I did was drink and raise hell. Oh, well, you don't have time to hear my life history. I just stopped to say hello and give you this.

He pulls folded bills from his shirt pocket. He sticks them out the window.

I can't take it, I say, thinking only a split second later that all this walking must've jarred my brain loose. Since when does anybody in his right mind turn down free money? Me and my big mouth.

Now, you look here, he says. I *want* to give this to you. It's not much, but it would mean something to me. Now, here, take it.

Thanks, I say, easing the money into my pocket. You said you're a singer?

While his left elbow rests on his open window and his right hand grips the steering wheel of his new Cadillac, he begins to sing *Amazing Grace*. Yes, sir, I like the way this thing called TV works. You appear on it one day and the next people stop to give you money and sing a song. I'm not so amused, however, as his eyes begin to water with the words, . . . *a wretch like me. I once was lost and now I'm found* . . .

I'm still a bit choked up as I watch his big shiny car disappear over the hill to the west. As when I saw the man with the rock, I know I have witnessed only the tip of the iceberg. I'm not sure I wanted him to tell me more about himself. I didn't want to see him totally break down and cry. It might've taken me too close to my own sadness.

I use the money that evening to get a room in Mansfield, at the Mimosa Motel. I'm not hurting for a shower or a bed. But I was interviewed by another TV station from Springfield today and I want to see how the piece is handled on the air. Ah, yes, there's my persona on the screen now. It is telling America how four thousand Cherokee died on the Trail of Tears and that what it is doing has no pretense at being the same as what the Indians experienced. Concise, clean, and to the point—like the camera shots. But that's the *persona* talking. I—the real me—was thinking: There's a lot of dirty, greedy bastards in this country who'll take anything they can get their hands on just like they did 150 years ago when they screwed the Indians. Watch 'em, and watch 'em close, because they use this very invention I'm on right now to brainwash you into believing you need a new car or a new this or that to be somebody. They don't give a shit about who you are or how you feel. They want you to work your ass off week after week so they can drain you of every red cent. The more they please you with their programs, the more in debt you get to become their slave.

Okay, okay, so I'm getting a bit wound up. But so what? If a man can't do that from time to time, he's either much more highly evolved than me or he's given up. But enough of this, let's go outside and see if anybody recognizes my persona.

I sit on a bench in front of the motel and take off my shoes and socks. I'm busy rubbing my feet when two old women come from the room behind me.

Ya'll doing okay today? I say.

They eye me as if I want something. They aren't sure whether to answer or not. I could be putting the move on 'em for a little necking. The smaller one decides to live on the wild side.

We're a bit tired, she says. We were driving all day.

I know the feeling, I say. I've been walking all day.

*Walking?* says the bigger one.

I get right to the point.

We're following a historic route ourselves, she says. We drove to Wisconsin from Michigan where we live and then on to the Dakotas.

We're tracing the life of Laura Ingalls Wilder, says the smaller one. She wrote the books that became the *Little House on the Prairie* series.

She lived here in Mansfield, says the other, when she wrote them. That's why we're here. Her house has been turned into a museum.

We're the ones who got the series on television, says the smaller one.

*Well,* says the other, I don't think—

*We did,* says her friend. We were teaching at the time and saw how much the children loved Laura Wilder's books. We wrote to Hollywood and told them.

# CHAPTER EIGHTEEN

THE NEXT MORNING is off to a curious start inside the Mimosa Motel. While I shave I turn on the TV, and guess what, the station happens to be showing, yep, that's it, *Little House on the Prairie*. Well, yeah, stranger things have happened, but stay tuned, folks. Things are just warming up in the Coincidence Department.

I kiss the Mimosa Motel adios and head for the other side of town to see Laura Ingalls Wilder's home. When I spot a phone outside a grocery store, I stop to call the newspaper office. I'm disturbed to find a dead hummingbird. Its beak is stuck in a crack in the top of the phone box. I've never seen a hummingbird this close up and it's as delicate as its magical flight. I think of Dan in Oklahoma City, who told his bird story about e. e. cummings. I also see the mayor of Proctor at the grocery store, where two feeders buzz with these beauties. I take the bird from the box and lay it in my hand. Its body is still warm. Who killed it and why did he stick the body here? I ease the tip of my index finger toward the back of the bird. When I touch it, I see the face of Dr. Noble, a member of the Bird Clan, back in Tahlequah. A part of me wants to bury my dead friend. Another part of me says *put it back where you found it.* I obey.

The first time the number doesn't work, so I fish the quarter from the tray to deposit it again. A man with a notebook arrives and watches as if he's in a hurry.

I'll only be a second, I say.

I try the number again, but I get no answer. I hang up the phone and slip into my pack again. The man with the notebook continues to study me.

It's all yours, I say.

I wanted to see *you,* he says. I'm from the paper.

Is it just another coincidence, or have I entered some kind of unusual realm here in the Ozarks around Mansfield, Missouri? The reporter explains that he was driving by and just happened to see me and my pack. But it's a third chance happening, yet to come by dark, which really makes me scratch my head.

When the reporter completes a short interview, I march on into the sleepy town. My face got sunburned yesterday and I'm afraid of skin cancer. I enter a variety store to get some sunscreen.

No, says the cashier. We don't have any. You might check across the street.

This is simple enough, but a woman a few feet away turns to eye me as if she wants to say something. She looks Indian and stands almost five feet, ten inches tall. I've never seen eyes like hers. They're grayish blue and seemed charged with more energy than she knows what to do with. She's about twenty-five and her lips are as thick and moist as mine are thin and sunburned. I feel a connection with her, and I don't know why I don't say hello. I head on out the door.

Laura Ingalls Wilder's house is one mile east of town. It sits on a hill among oaks and a stream flows at its base. I tour the roped-off rooms and smell the same old wooden floors and beams as Laura Wilder smelled when she was unknowingly writing a TV series. Anyway, it's a charming old country home and I'm sure that the two aging schoolteachers from Michigan will now go to their graves with more peace in their hearts.

I wander into the gift shop. Five female Mennonites browse through books by Laura Ingalls Wilder, and I'm careful not to make eye contact with the one who is pretty and about my age. I'm afraid that she might see the lust in my eyes and punch me in the name of God. I'm intrigued with their clothes, for they wear no buttons or zippers. Everything is held together with straight pins. I wonder if I haven't entered a part of America made up of religious groups, for yesterday I saw five horse-drawn buggies driven by Amish men. By waving my arm nearly off, I finally managed to get one driver to stop.

You won't drive a car? I said.

No, no, he said. I won't drive a car.

Why? I said.

God doesn't want us to go so fast, he said. If we did, how could we see what is around us?

But don't cars and planes carry medicine to save lives? I said.

They do, he said. But then, how many people have they killed as well?

Do you have electricity in your home? I said.

No, he said. Why should I? What can it show me that a

candle or my imagination can't? It might show me things I don't want in my mind. Are you *walking*?

Yes, I said. I don't believe in riding, even in your buggy. You go too fast.

His stoic expression finally gave way to a warm smile and he offered his hand. I'll remember his grip as long as I live. It was warm and strong like a hand that knew its place in a crazy world.


Susan, the woman who runs the gift shop, wants to phone the leader of a nearby commune. She thinks he'll be interested in showing me around this part of the country.

What kind of commune? I say.

Oh, she says, it's nothing like you've seen before. Their houses have been created from visions and they live close to the earth.

A hippie commune? I say.

Well, she says, in a way. But not really. Shall I phone the leader?

I have visions of Jim Jones as the leader and it makes me uneasy, to say the least. The last thing I want right now is to be preached at by someone who swears that he's found the golden path. On the other hand, Susan seems like a woman who cares about what I'm doing. She wouldn't, I hope, deliver me into the hands of some fanatics. Besides, I began this journey, in part, to see what's happening with Americans across the country. I can't afford to be a candy-ass about meeting folks just because they have a different lifestyle than I do.

They have a lot of Indian blood, says Susan. If that helps you decide about meeting them.

She phones the leader and he arrives some twenty minutes

later. Nathan Kilgore is in his late fifties and walks with a slight limp. A knot sticks from his right knee where he recently hurt it doing farmwork. He wears a hat and a mustache. His eyes are bright and clear, but a slight gut sticks over his belt.

Sorry to stare, I say. But you look so much like a Gypsy chief I spent the day with in Mexico that you could pass for brothers.

Nathan breaks into one of the most beautiful and contagious laughs I've ever heard. His face lights up and his whole body shakes. Santa Claus himself might envy his jolly radiance. He agrees to drive me around the area to see where the Amish live and I load my pack into his old dusty Buick.

Susan wasn't very clear, I say, on what kind of commune you lead?

It's not what people think, he says. We don't share wives or husbands and we don't drink or do drugs. There's about fifty of us now and we try to live in peace. There was almost one hundred of us, but just what happened is another story I'll tell you later. We're descendants of the Sioux and the Ute. Would you like to spend the night and see for yourself how we live?

Yes, I say. I would.

But the words are hardly out of my mouth when I become anxious. This is not like me, to accept an invitation so quickly when it means I'll be in the middle of a group. Nathan seems like a warm and loving person, but what if he's something else under the surface? What if his group tries to brainwash me into seeing the world the way they do? I'm not afraid that they'll succeed, but what a mess to get out of if they try. I can be polite for just so long till my darker side wants to strike out. I should've simply thanked him and said I'd play it by ear after seeing where the Amish live.

Does your group have a name? I say.

Yes, he laughs. We call ourselves 'Zion's Order.'

You organized it?

No, he says. My father did that some forty years ago. He's dead now. Both him and Mother. They died last year. The group started back in Utah, he laughs. My father led a caravan of trucks and cars all the way to Mexico looking for the right spot to settle down. We finally found ourselves here in the Ozarks. We did have seventeen hundred acres. Now we've got twelve hundred. We had to give five hundred acres to our lawyer when he defended our case in the Supreme Court. But like I said, that's a story for later.

As Nathan talks I have a greater sense that his Santa Claus laughter stems from the same swan-and-lily spring where hurts and scars crawl about on the shaded bottom like hungry leeches. I'm about to ask about the story concerning the Supreme Court when we pull from the highway onto a dirt road, dust rising and drifting into the car to make me cough and sneeze. The dust also mixes with the sunscreen and runs into my eyes to make them burn and tear. I'm rubbing them with my handkerchief when I think of the tall Indian woman with the grayish blue eyes I saw in the variety store. I wish she were driving me around the Ozarks.


Two-story Amish farmhouses cover the rolling hills, where gardens are orange with pumpkins. Ducks, chickens, and geese wander about the barnyards while workers drive horse-drawn machines, baling hay. The sky around the houses is refreshingly clean of telephone poles, and windmills twirl in the autumn wind. A young woman, hanging out clothes, returns a hardy wave as we turn a curve to find eight or ten schoolchildren in the middle of the road. The boys wear hats and carry their shoes in their hands as if their feet had refused to take another step till they touched the dirt, letting it play in their toes. As we ease on down the road the children hop to the side, their faces alive with after-school freedom.

Do the Amish *never* ride in cars? I say.

They ride in 'em, laughs Nathan. They just refuse to own or operate them.

Isn't that a little hypocritical?

Nathan simply offers his famous laugh as we pull back onto the highway, where a bearded driver hurries his horse and buggy onto the dirt road. It's as though the asphalt marks the boundary between two worlds—past and present. I'm intrigued that both worlds exist. It scares me to think I would have to live in a single one. In fact, that's what I find so rich about America: it's many worlds at once.

*There's* a good chicken house, says Nathan.

A *good* one?

He's one of our customers, says Nathan. That's one of the ways we support ourselves. We have a chicken crew. We catch, de-beak, and vaccinate chickens to be shipped to market.

Why do you de-beak them?

Well, says Nathan, if you don't, they'll peck each other to death. They got a thing about blood. Once they taste it, they can't stop. Before we got into the chicken business, we cut firewood and sold it to pay for the land. It was a lot cheaper back thirty years ago. Then the Amish came down from Pennsylvania with cash some ten years later and drove the prices way up.

Some five miles south of Mansfield we take a dirt road up a hill that's so rough that even the big Buick bounces about. Minutes later, back in what seems the middle of nowhere, we come to an arched sign:

WELCOME TO ZION'S ORDER
COME IN PEACE
STAY IN PEACE
GO IN PEACE

The faded sign is coming apart and vines grow around it. I wonder why Nathan and his order don't give it a face-lift. We turn at the sign and a village appears in the distance. It makes me think of a town built after an atomic bomb. The houses are made of tin, wood, and rock and put together as if the builders followed blueprints drawn by children. One is in the shape of an ark and another is a dome and is as big as a barn. Atop it is a tower.

That's our chapel, says Nathan. We built the tower when the war within the group broke out.

# CHAPTER NINETEEN

A THIRD HOUSE LOOKS like a giant dollhouse with a massive rock chimney. TV antennas tower above other houses and wires seem to go everywhere. Vines cover some of the porches and climb over the roofs. The house where Nathan and his family live sports the largest chimney I've ever seen. It reaches above surrounding trees and reminds me of the Leaning Tower of Pisa. Rope-thick wires are fastened to its top and secured on the ground. The whole village looks as though it could collapse at any second, and yet, that's what I find magical about it. It's the human spirit caught in junk lumber, rock, and metal, with the modern world—TV antennas and telephone wires—wrapped around it. It's what a group of aspiring purists or misfits call home. I'm not yet sure if I'm amused or saddened.

An old woman wearing a big red hat comes from a building

made of wooden slabs that sits between the chapel and the house designed like an ark. A rope dangles from a giant rusty bell atop a ten-foot pole at the corner of the building.

That's our dining hall, says Nathan. We also use the bell as a fire alarm. Wasn't long ago somebody set a fire down in the woods and it was blazing this way, straight for the chapel. We all got down on our knees in a prayer circle and the wind changed direction. It was good for the young ones to see the power of the Lord firsthand.

The old woman in the red hat continues to eye me, an outsider. I try to break the ice.

I sure like that hat, I say.

Thank you, she says. Nathan, could I see you when you have time? Won't take long.

Excuse me, he says.

He joins the old woman some thirty feet away and they whisper as if all secrets must be kept within the tribe. My brain buzzes with intrigue. What's the war Nathan spoke of that forced them to build the tower on the chapel? Who set the fire he claims was stopped by circle prayer, and what is the old woman whispering about?

My father built the house we lived in when I was born. Downstairs, he and Mother ran a grocery store. We moved when I was four and the building was sold to a religious group which handled rattlesnakes to prove its faith. I pass that old home every time I drive to the gym to work out. I can't see it without thinking of snakes crawling where I learned to walk and talk. I wonder what rituals Zion's Order practices to show its faith? The old woman finally nods and heads for the dwelling that looks like a big dollhouse. Nathan joins me.

Sorry to keep you waiting, he says. Her sink is leaking and I'm in charge of repairs.

He laughs yet again and I'm not sure whether to believe him or not. A truck arrives and several people come from it. I do a double take: It's the woman I admired in the variety store. This time she offers a smile and a handshake.

This is my niece, Venda, he says.

Glad to meet you, she says, and disappears into the house in the shape of an ark.

What kind of name is 'Venda'? I say.

My father named her, says Nathan. He named most of his grandchildren. The names came to him in visions, like the shapes of our houses. He was a lawyer and a chiropractor. He wrote songs too. Over one thousand of them. We sing them when we meet on Sunday. You want to see our chapel?

As I follow him up the stairs I turn to see if I can get another glimpse of Venda. I don't know how, but I'm determined to talk to her. She not only intrigues me, she excites me in all the right places. I'm disappointed that I don't find her peeking from the window of the ark. Then it hits me: She's probably married.

Nathan holds the door open for me to enter the chapel. I've seen the great cathedrals of Europe, but they don't compare to what I feel here. Every wall is bursting alive with paintings so rich in color and composition that they seem inspired. One shows two Indians on horses as they overlook a great valley. Another offers a family walking among bears and lions and lambs. A boy plays in the grass with a snake while a nearby garden prospers with vegetables and fruit trees. My favorite captures another family awed by a shower of shooting stars over a desert of camels.

Instead of wooden pews, chairs and couches are scattered about the chapel as if honoring God should be a comfortable and joyous occasion. An old ceiling fan twirls overhead and a dove coos from a cage. It strikes me that this would be a perfect place to spend the night. I want to sleep on one of the couches and light a candle to flicker on the painting with the meteor shower.

Well, Nathan says, there's only one problem with that. Two single women live here. On either end of the chapel, that is. They might not be comfortable. I thought you might enjoy the room me and my wife had picked out for you at our place. It's made from the old milk barn from the Laura Ingalls Wilder farm.

Yes, indeed, the two old Michigan schoolteachers can eat their hearts out now.

What are *those*? I say, pointing to another painting. They look like three flying saucers.

We've seen 'em for years, he says. We believe they guard the planet. It's nothing we argue about with others. Either people believe or they don't. Actually, we try to keep the sightings to ourselves. We're not here to put on a show. A while back we also found burned spots in a field that looked like where a craft had landed.

He leads me into a back room where his mother and father slept. Nathan, the first of six children, is pictured with his parents when he was a baby. Next to that picture is the classical drawing of Jesus walking on water with a caption reading LIFE ETERNAL. Above that is a third picture, where an angel with enormous wings floats over two children crossing a bridge. The building, I'm told, is the remains of an old dairy. Electricity was added when it became a home and a chapel; wires, running atop the wooden walls, bend and twist like vines connecting sockets and lights. The soothing coo of the caged dove is disrupted by the dinner bell.

I'm not only starved, I'm hopeful that I'll get to see Venda again. We leave the angel and the flying saucers, to descend on food.

\* \* \*

Two swinging doors open to the dining room, where a table ten feet long is loaded with food. I grab a plate and follow Nathan down the line, where we serve ourselves with tossed salad, potatoes, and rolls made from wheat raised and ground here on the ranch. Pitchers, resting on nearby tables where we sit, are filled with well water.

It's hard for us to drink city water, says Nathan. We taste the chlorine.

The room is filled with laughter as well as the dings of knives and forks against plates. The children, smiling and curious about the outsider, radiate healthy glows. I'm surprised to discover a couple with rotten spots on their teeth. I'm caught between feeling sorry for them and being repulsed.

You've fallen into a crazy bunch here, says Nathan's sister, Barbara, who begins to laugh.

I knew there was something about it I liked, I say, joining her laughter, but perhaps too loudly.

Crazy for *Jesus,* she adds, her lips tightening.

Finally, I spot Venda in the food line. When our eyes connect, she comes toward my end of the table. But she takes only three or four steps before she turns back to sit as far away as possible. I don't get it.

On the wall is a framed photograph as big as a poster. It was taken for a newspaper story back in the fifties, when Zion's Order first settled here. It shows the group on winter's barren hillside. A child rides on the shoulder of Marl Kilgore, the founder, as the others follow and carry more children in cradles made of poles and leather. A dog that could pass for Lassie's twin plays alongside. It strikes me with a sense of hope against a mountain of despair. They look as though they have been walking for days in search of the Promised Land. Nathan was a teenager, standing tall and thin at the founder's side.

I wish you could've met my father, says Nathan.

The weight and tone of his words convince me just how much Nathan loved his father and how he misses him. I also gather that he fears he isn't filling the old man's shoes as leader.

I wish I could've talked to your father, I say. What happened to his dream?

Well, says Nathan, lowering his head, we founded Zion's Order with the hope of building a community where we could simply live in peace, like Christ's apostles. We shared all the work and pooled our money. We believed in love, and still do, and that all things were possible with God's help as long as we had faith. But—he takes a deep breath—some of my brothers and sisters began to lose faith in the Order and wanted their share of the land for their own use. It became a power struggle over who should be the leader, and we had to ask them to leave. It broke my father's heart. It became a war. Brother turned against brother. One night our fence post shop was bombed and a few nights later we found some fifteen people with torches sneaking through the woods. They wanted to burn the Order to the ground. I shot over their heads and scared them away. That's when we built the tower over the chapel, Nathan continues. For five years we guarded the ranch day and night with dogs and guns. We finally ended up in the Supreme Court in a battle with our own brothers and sisters. But it didn't end there. The unfaithful are still trying to destroy us. They sent a blind man to join our group. He donated some money and then claimed we cheated him. We had to go to court with him. We later discovered that he had swindled an old woman out of four hundred thousand dollars in California. We can't be too careful anymore. They're out to get us.

The story makes me wonder where reality ends and delusion

begins. I've always gotten along so well with my two sisters that I find it difficult to imagine such a war within a family. I see how it could make a man walk on eggshells as he looks over his shoulder.

Nathan shows me around the ranch, and we begin in the kitchen where the food is cooked in an enormous wood-burning stove. The air in the walk-in cooler is rich with the smell of red apples, stacked in washtubs. They get milk from their own cows and gallon jars float with thick cream; butter will be made in the morning. An old school bus has had its tires removed and now serves as a place to dry fruits and vegetables. The garden spot, as big as a football field, isn't a happy sight. It's overgrown with weeds and a scarecrow, standing in the center, has lost a lot of its straw stuffing. It's a ghost of old faded jeans and a red shirt. Its hat has slipped down over its eyes as if it doesn't want to see anymore.

Our gardener of twenty years died this summer, says Nathan. I'm not sure who'll take over his job. None of us knows as much about it as he did.

Nathan's brother, Douglas, is one of three priests here in the Order. He drives a truck, usually loaded with chickens, and it's now being repaired in their well-equipped garage by another brother, Harry. Another building, constructed from lumber salvaged from a fire in town, houses a trampoline where children bounce and twirl in midair.

Down at the barn, a blind calf bumps into the fence. He was given to the children by a neighbor and will be used as a breeding bull when he's older. Yet another shed holds pigeons, flying about and cooing as if to show off.

*  *  *

When I was twelve, I climbed a tree and took a young
pigeon from its nest. That bird was my life that summer, a bridge
between girls and Nature. I held it every day and stroked its
growing wings. When I fed it, I was startled to find a rare whistle
coming from my lips. It was as gentle and warm as breath itself.
My only claim to musical fame, I whistled the song to the bird till
it was trained. No matter where it was, in a tree or atop a house, I
could blow the secret little tune and it would leap into the sky to
dive for my arm or shoulder. I can't swear that it kissed me, but it
would ease the tip of its beak against my cheeks and eyes as if I
were a lover. But I suppose relationships, in any form or fashion,
aren't meant to last forever. When the bird was two years old—it
turned out to be female and once built a nest in an old ice-cream
freezer hanging in the barn—I went to Florida with my family to
play in the ocean and get sunburned. When we returned, I
couldn't find my feathered friend. I whistled to trees. I whistled to
houses and barns. I finally found the feathers on the ground
where a dog or cat obeyed Nature's Laws. Sometimes even today
I'll find myself whistling that old song. I almost expect the sky to
come alive with that bird, floating down to my arm to kiss my
cheeks and eyes.


On the west side of the ranch a dirt road leads through the
woods to the Order's swimming pool. It was dug by hand and
poured with concrete. It's now empty except for a little tobacco-
colored water collecting autumn leaves. Wild turkey tracks lead
from the holy pool.

Back up in the woods some two hundred yards from the
water sit Healing Rock and Holy Rock. This is where the faithful

come to seek divine help. On more than one occasion God is said to have granted a vision to show the way.

The dirt road circles back to the east toward the ranch to pass the Order's cemetery. Some ten graves haunt the ground and there's room for more. One of the graves was dug up and the body was taken into town for an autopsy. One of the unfaithful who had left the Order swore to the local authorities that the leader had killed the young woman.

He locked her in a room, said the unfaithful, and starved her to death.

It was a lie, says Nathan. The autopsy proved that the woman died of cancer.

The dirt road leads past a pile of junk cars, rusty bicycles, and dead farm machinery. Dozens of walnut trees, their branches bending from thousands of nuts, line the road as we once again enter the village. On an outside concrete floor, David, the third and last priest of the Order, disassembles a TV. Several more are stacked behind him. Of course, anyone can appoint himself to any post in his own organization, but I find it so odd that a *priest* is working on a contraption as worldly as a TV. For all I know, David may be an MTV freak who likes to rock and roll when no one's watching.

Nothing wrong with TV, he says. It's a great invention. It's what is shown that I sometimes question.

I'm concerned about the fear TV puts into people, I say. You got one show after another showing murder and rape. People begin to believe that's the way most people are. It's disgusting because it warps reality to sell products. Most of the folks I've met have been warm and kind, but they keep telling me to be careful of the next guy. The next guy tells me the same thing. We don't have more movies on TV about humanity because people are becoming addicted to sensationalism. It's a form of drug as far as I'm concerned. Who are the dealers?

Nathan and I head for his house and I take my pack from his old Buick. As I do so I spy once again on the ark house where Venda lives. I'm tempted to ask Nathan about her, but I'm concerned he'll think I'm after her body. This isn't true. I'm interested in her mind, soul, *and* body—praise the Lord.

# CHAPTER TWENTY

THAT NIGHT NATHAN'S wife, Berna, makes chocolate-chip cookies. The six children and myself pig out as I read stories to the two youngest girls, Chana and Questel. As I send Jack over the candlestick and find Little Boy Blue fast asleep, I put my arms around the girls and pretend, for a few magnificent moments, that I'm their father.

We're really thankful, says Berna, to have you here in our home. We weren't so lucky with the last guest.

No, says Nathan. He set the house on fire.

I've heard so much intrigue by this point I don't know what to believe. It's not that I think they're lying to me. It's just that I'm not sure that they know the truth themselves.

You think he was sent to set the fire? I say.

I'm sure he was, says Nathan, breaking into his Santa Claus laughter. The fire started in the room where you're sleeping tonight. The heater had been there for years without a hint of trouble till he came. I had to ask him to leave.

I hope nothing happens while I'm here, I say, wondering if I'm not already on the suspect list.

No, says Berna. We see into people. You have a good spirit.

I'm thankful for the vote of confidence, but if the members of Zion's Order can truly see, how have they managed to get involved in so much chaos? For that matter, though, who the hell am I to dare judge them, when my own life hasn't exactly been a road lined with peach blossoms?

You make me feel at home, I say. Your children remind me how much I miss a family of my own sometimes.


Nathan and I go to visit his sister, Barbara, who lives with her husband and son in the same building with the chapel. She's in a rocking chair with her feet sticking across the floor like a character in a *Snuffy* comic strip. Her presence is anything but light, however. She weighs around two hundred pounds and her shoulders and arms look like they could chop down a tree in nothing flat. As she rocks, her fingers work a needle and thread to sew patches on a quilt.

Ever saw one like this? she says.

She spreads the quilt on the floor and I'm captivated because all the patches are made of sweaters. They make simple but truly unique designs.

No, I say, I haven't. Is this your idea?

Yes, she says with a modest tone. I sent one to a store in New York. They wrote back and said they wouldn't have such a thing in their shop.

You wait and see, I say. In time, these quilts will be big collector's items.

It takes so little sometimes to make people feel good about themselves. She pulls the quilt back into her lap and begins to sew again. Her eyes have warmed and one of her bare feet now does a subtle little jig. Ah, yes, this thing called human contact is something else.


When Nathan and I start back to his house, I suggest that he go on inside without me. I want to savor this village beneath the stars so I can better remember it when my teeth begin to fall out. Also, I just plain old need a break from being around people. A loner by nature, I must periodically let my mind do as it likes. Tonight my spirit follows it up into the wood smoke rising from the chimneys. It drifts across the moon and settles atop the walnut trees near the graveyard. I'm tempted to walk to Holy Rock and Healing Rock, but fear I could be mistaken as the unfaithful and shot in the dark. A light is on in the ark and I'd love to talk to Venda to see if I'm simply caught in a passing dream or if we have a real connection. This is the second highest hill in this part of the Ozarks and the view is spectacular. Lights of farmhouses twinkle for so many miles in the great distance that they blend with the stars. It's easy to imagine that this is Heaven and all is right with the world. A miracle has happened and there's no more doubt or pain. The paintings in the chapel have come alive. Men, women, and children now walk among the lambs and the lions. But the lights of a truck now come down the road and Heaven vanishes in a cloud of nightly dust. The only thing that remains is the dove, cooing in the chapel. Then, as I begin to walk, even that disappears.

* * *

When I enter Nathan's house, some of the children are watching *Matlock* on TV. Chana, the youngest girl at five, carries a parrot on her hand. She places it on my shoulder and laughs as if she's placed a lock on me and wants to see if I can escape.

If you don't like *Matlock,* says Lasha, we have a new *Three Stooges* tape.

What's that on your shoulder? says Chana.

Ever since I arrived the children have been so warm and friendly that I almost suspect they've been taught to be this way to lure new members into the Order. But I decide I'm simply so on guard that my imagination is working overtime. I take the parrot from my shoulder and Chana sits beside me on the couch with a daring little grin.

Can he talk? I say.

No, she says. But he listens.

I go to bed with a peace and calm some men might kill for. There are no outside lights here and the stars are so bright they seem to sit right on the window sills. I wouldn't be totally surprised right now for a flying saucer to float down from the heavens. It's so quiet I think I could almost hear a feather drop. Indeed, I *do* hear a song, gently echoing of the day.

I hear Nathan up at the crack of dawn. He gathers with the workers in the chapel to discuss today's goals, just who'll do what. I finally roll out of bed around eight and load my pack. I'm invited to stay as long as I like, but I have over six hundred miles yet to go and I want to get home before winter comes.

I'm about to leave the house when Chana appears with her impish grin. I squat and she melts into my arms. It's almost more than I can bear without crying. When Nathan and I get outside, I put on my sunglasses to hide my eyes. I don't want anyone to see how much I'm feeling. I couldn't live like these folks, but I'm knocked out by their dream, however fragile, to work and live in peace side by side.

As Nathan and I drive away from the village I take one last look at the ark where Venda lives. I cushion myself with that old cliché, Some things just aren't meant to be.

Nathan takes me back to Laura Wilder's home, where we met. I don't know when or why, but my gut tells me we'll meet again. With his laughter still warm in my ears, I hit the Trail.

# CHAPTER TWENTY-ONE

T HE MAN WITH the rock is the only person on foot I've met on the Trail till now. A quarter mile ahead of me a man approaches with a small bag strapped over his shoulder. He wears a cap and walks with a hurried bounce. He isn't thumbing and he isn't picking up cans to hustle a few bucks. I'm not afraid of him, but I can't get the man with the rock out of my mind. What does this man have in his bag? Why is he out here on the Trail? As we get closer I see his trimmed red beard, and I can now make out that LUCKY is written across the front of his cap. His eyes squint as much as mine as we come within a few feet of each other.

Where are you going? I say.

California, he says. Where are *you* going?

Alabama, I say. What's happening in California?

Gold, he says. I'm looking for gold. I did it a few years back too. But it was no good. Things are different now. I know I'll find it because I got faith now. You can do anything if you got the faith. I never met another walker before. You're the first, and I been doing it since I was eleven years old. I like to walk. You see more things and I can sleep in the woods. Sometimes I build me a fire to stay warm. Sometimes people take me in. Like last night, I got into Willow Springs and went to the police station. You know, to let 'em know I was in town. Some preacher there got me a motel room on his credit card. See, I got faith. Walking's good, but don't do it at night. That's when the bad spirits come out, because they think people can't see 'em. Walk in the daytime. Walk in the light.

You're walking all the way to California? I say.

If I have to, he says. I don't mind. A sister lives over here in Mansfield. I'll stop there and rest. Maybe get me a couple days of work before I push on.

Eddy and his Lucky cap hurry on down the road. From time to time I turn to see how far he's getting. I wish I had given him my address to keep me informed about the gold strike. After all, a fellow walker might want to share his empire. Shoot, I missed the boat again.

I stop for lunch in a truck stop and catch up on my journal, only to run into unwelcome news. The man eating in the booth two seats over says his wife used to be a social worker in the area.

Zion's Order? he says, when I tell him where I've come from. Everybody in this area knows about *them*. My wife says they got a lot of calls about child abuse down there.

I don't buy it, I say. They may be a bit off-center compared to us, who are so damn sure of ourselves, but I saw nothing but tenderness with their children.

Okay, says the man. I'm not writing it in blood. I'm just telling you what I've heard.

A short man wanders over to my table and turns his back so no one can see his hands. I'm not sure what to expect.

I been hearing ya'll talk, he says, about that walk and all. I'm from Alabama myself. Drive that truck parked out yonder.

He may be as redneck as I am on a bad day, but his hand eases forward with the grace of a gentleman wearing a white glove. Fingers open to a rolled bill. I shake my head.

Now, which is it, he says. Are you that broke or just so high and mighty that one Southerner can't help another? Hell, son, it ain't charity. It's a contribution.

I've had a love-hate relationship with Alabama since I was seventeen and ran away to New York one summer to get out from under the tobacco juice, grits, racism, and my own lack of understanding and tolerance. I can't say I'd kiss every cheek in the state today. But whether I like it or not, and I do, I always feel a bond with another soul from Dixie when I'm hundreds of miles from home. I need the money this good old boy holds in his hand. But I don't take it for myself, though I can be as greedy as the next guy, as much as I do to honor the look in his eyes.

When you get back to Alabama, I say, tell 'em I'm coming. I may be crawling when I get there, but I'm on the way.

Hurricane Hugo blasted the South Carolina coast a couple of days ago and the Ozarks begin to get cold winds. I'm chilling when I finally find a place to camp at dusk. It's near a pond and I pitch my tent as a frog begins to croak. I build a fire and sit as close to it as possible. I don't mind the smoke. It takes me back to last night at Zion's Order, when I stood alone to watch other smoke carry me into Heaven. I can't kick what the man said in the truck stop about child abuse at the ranch. Even rumors often have roots in truth.

I break a branch from a cedar. The Cherokee, like many other tribes, considered this tree sacred, because it stayed green in winter. Though the wood was too precious to burn, the green twigs were sometimes dropped into a fire as incense. The smell could drive away evil ghosts from dreams.

Scalp trophies were sometimes hung on a cedar while the warrior danced about with them dangling overhead. The tree's red color may have come from the blood of an evil magician who once changed the course of the sun. Two warriors cut off his head and hung it atop a cedar tree; the red dripped down the branches and trunk.

I break twigs from the cedar branch. One by one I drop them into the flames, where they crackle and pop as if alive with spirits taking flight into trees and stars. The Cherokee often said their prayers while sitting by a fire because they felt that the smoke carried them to Heaven. I do the same as the night grows colder and the moon appears.

I curl up in my sleeping bag with the exotic smell of evergreen on my hands. The frog's croak becomes so soft that I actually can't determine, at times, if the sound comes from the pond, or if my guts are growling. I have trouble getting to sleep and I can't get warm. I keep turning from one side to the other in search of the womb.

A coyote howls to my right and another answers to my left. The comforting hoot of an owl fails to come and I hear something walking in the woods. It sounds as big as a man and I once again picture the man with the rock. No, I decide, it's a dog. Not a wild one, I hope. The snap of branches jars the night and I convince myself it's a bear. It's easy to be a warrior while watching a movie or facing a gym mirror to pump iron, but out here in the woods in the middle of nowhere is another story. I'm tempted to growl like the meanest son-of-a-bitch alive and see if whatever it is will run like hell. I end up following the path of the frog and staying as quiet as a heartbeat. Finally, after I've been eaten alive two or three times, the "bear" changes directions to fade into the night.

I awake with a nightmare. No, it's not a dream. It's real and I knew it would happen while I'm on the walk. My father has died. Yes, I'm sure of it. The feeling is too great to be anything but a psychic connection. I've only had two like this in my entire life, and I was right both times. Now I must lie here in the cold for hours as I await dawn to pack and walk for who knows how many miles to find a phone to confirm this horror.

It gets colder and I'm haunted by memories of my father. I once sneaked his fiddle from our house to show other boys and girls in the woods and we accidentally broke it into pieces. When I was five, I threw a hunting knife at my cousin, Gary, the one who lives across the road from me and disappeared six months ago. It pierced his cheek just below his right eye. My father whipped me with his belt as he dragged me to the car where I curled up into a ball on the floorboard and cried in shame.

Then there was the time my father and I walked across a great sagebrush field to sit under a tree. With his knife, he carved me a knife from a hickory limb. It was almost a foot long and fit my hand perfectly. I knew that, somehow, he had put magic into that knife. When we walked back across the sagebrush field, I swung the wooden blade before me to clear the way of bad men and monsters. What I'd give to hold that knife just now as I fear the worst, going to my father's funeral. I wish the Little People would sneak up from the woods and put me to sleep with a soothing dream. I wish I were home.

* * *

When morning comes I find that I'm in a delicate ice cave. Sunlight filters through the heavy frost on my sagging tent. I have no gloves and my hands freeze as I roll up the nylon and stuff it into its bag. Spooks in the night are supposed to evaporate in daylight, but I'm still convinced that my father died.

I walk miles before I find a phone at a run-down gas station. I phone home and the rings go on and on. I'm about to hang up when my mother finally answers. I'm the happiest man alive when she tells me everything is fine. Yes, a human being can be resurrected.

I stay high for hours from the good news concerning my father, but my body finally begins to tire and I drop in the woods on a pile of leaves. I was hasty to leave Zion's Order. I should've stayed another night and given my body a chance to rest. I pull out my map of Missouri. It's as wrinkled as the face of a hundred-year-old man. Like my canteen and the campfire, it has almost taken on human qualities. I'm reassured when it's in my hand. However manmade and contrived are its red lines and blue and green patches, it's still a constant companion and always ready to give all of itself. When I spot Current River a hundred miles away running through the middle of Van Buren, it strikes me that this will make an ideal spot to hold over for a couple of days to rest and enjoy the water.

Inspired by the thought of reaching Current River, I fold the map and start that way. I walk less than a mile when a magnificent crane glides over me. Its grace and beauty feed me such a sense of magic that I begin to chant.

There's a story the Cherokee told about a crane and a hummingbird in love with the same beautiful Cherokee woman. She considered the crane homely. She thought the hummingbird beautiful. Believing the hummingbird would win, she agreed to marry the one who won a race around the world. The humming-bird was so sure of himself that he rested at night while the slow but determined crane flew through the darkness. When the crane won the race, the pretty woman didn't honor her word. She refused to marry the crane. His long delicate neck quivered with rejection as his awkward body leaped for the sky. Some say he turned his pain into the beauty of his flight.

I continue to chant as I watch the crane disappear over the treetops. I take it as a good omen and walk no more than five minutes till a car pulls over with a hand waving as if the owner is a friend. I can tell it's a woman, but the sun is in my eyes and I can't imagine who it is. I walk that way and discover, as surely as if the crane announced her, that it's Venda. I stare in disbelief and recall the night I danced around the fire after seeing the first crane. That same wondrous passion now stirs within me and I want to do a more private and sensuous dance meant for two.

I was hoping to see you, she says.

The reserve she showed in the dining hall two nights ago has vanished. Her eyes are inviting and her smile could charm the devil himself. I slip from the pack and squat beside her door like a desert nomad who's lucked upon the shade of a palm.

What are you doing out here? I say.

I had loom lessons all day, she says, over in Willow Springs. Otherwise, I never travel this road. Sorry I wasn't so friendly the other night. I thought you might think I was too pushy. Sometimes people at the ranch mistake my friendliness as something else. I just like people, she adds, her lips staying parted just enough for me to savor the tip of her tongue. Are you really comfortable, squatted like a frog?

I get into the car and her body language changes. Her head is a bit lowered and her eyes become softer. Something about her sudden shyness makes her all the more alluring. I want to ease my arms around her so much I can't stand it. It doesn't have to be sex, I just need to feel her against me, to somehow know that I'm all here on the walk. Also, I sense that she wants to be held as if suffering from some great loss that isn't easy to talk about.

Were you born on the ranch? I say.

My grandfather delivered me, she says. I've been there my whole life. It hasn't always been easy. Especially the last two years. Since my head injury.

Her injury, I'm told, happened when she was working as head of the chicken crew. Chickens were being loaded twelve to a cage and ten cages were then stacked atop each other into a battery, a metal frame on rollers. Venda was inside the half-loaded semitrailer to position each new battery as it was rolled to her. She, and she alone, was to give orders as the crew of ten loaded the truck. But someone, without her knowledge, told the driver to pull up a few feet. When she felt the moving sensation, she snaked her head from behind one of the batteries to see what was happening. The truck stopped and threw her head into a line of batteries just in time to see a new one rolling her way with a thousand pounds. Her head was caught between the two and crushed. She was knocked out for several hours and bedridden for two months. She never went to the doctor, but the Order's three priests anointed her head with holy oil and asked God to heal her.

I've had a headache for two years, she says. Every few weeks it'll force me into bed. I can't lift anything or it makes me dizzy. I try to stay busy so I don't think about it. I miss working with the chicken crew. I got to meet new people that way. I was good too. I could beat any man on stuffing birds in the cages for shipping. We had contests and I always won. That's why I'm taking loom lessons. So I can do more with my time. I play the guitar and sing too. It helps me forget my head. Sometimes I go to the nursing home and entertain the old folks there. Some of them don't have anybody.

I'm always amazed how the human face seems to change as someone reveals himself. This is true now with Venda as she opens up. It's as though she's been starved for someone besides those at the Order to listen to her rage, pain, sadness, and dreams. She was married when she was nineteen and lost her first baby the following year.

I still see that baby, she says. I think he was born dead because I was so unhappily married. I got two boys now, five and six, and they're fine. I divorced their father four years ago. I don't usually talk this much. I can't talk to most people, but you're easy to talk to. I can't believe you showed up at the ranch after I saw you in the store in Mansfield.

She smiles now as if talking has freed her, at least for a while, from all her worries. If she's used me just to spit out her poison, I don't care. I feel needed, and watching her lips and eyes are medicine for me. But, no, it's much more than that. She has that rare power to flame my lust while touching my heart at the same time. As the talk slows, we're forced to taste each other between the lines. We both realize the sadness, too, of my just passing through.

I'd better move on, I say.

Yeah, she whispers. You have a long way to go.

Could I hold you before I leave? I say.

Mmmm. She moans, sliding closer.

I ease my arms around her and smell her neck, warm where her hair's been thick against her skin. My cheek presses against hers and I hear her tender moans, deep down inside where her own lust builds near where her first baby died. My fingers stroke her back and are tempted to slide down to her hips. But they don't. I don't kiss her, either, for it's as though it would be almost too much to walk away from. We're still sitting, but our thighs manage to touch. Her arms are strong and not afraid to squeeze and pull me into her breasts. I'm tempted to ease my hand up her thigh and really let go. Instead, I find my fingers in her hair around a knot from the injury. I hold it for a moment before I kiss her cheek and back away.

I've got to go, I whisper, holding her hand.

Yes, she says, and begins to cry. Give me some of your strength, she adds, squeezing my hand.

I don't feel strong at all as I walk on. I do, however, begin to grasp a little about why this route is called the Trail of Tears. I turn to watch Venda drive away. She waves as she did when I first saw her today. I wave back and she disappears down the road. I'm caught between the great flight of the crane minutes before she appeared and the dead hummingbird with its delicate beak stuck in the phone box when I entered Mansfield. I have felt better.

# CHAPTER TWENTY-TWO

A KNOT APPEARS IN the crow's-foot of my right eye, where the tick had buried its head back in Tahlequah. That happened so long ago that I assumed I was free of any danger from the bite. I'm a little spooked that it may spell trouble.

For three days now I have a fever, but it's not the kind caused by a tick bite. It's a longing that stretches from the thighs up to the mouth, watering as I think of Venda and how good it felt to hold her in my arms. She rides on the owl's hoot at night to enter my dreams, and she soars with the crows and hawks by day to tease my thoughts. At the moment, I don't give a damn if I am a romantic fool. I want her as much as I ever wanted any woman in my life—and believe me, I've been so on fire a time or two it's a wonder I didn't go up in smoke. Indeed, I'm sure more than one person whispered that I needed to be hit with a bucket of water.

I once read a story about an old Cherokee, Tsali, who had more than just romantic passion for his wife. As the story goes, Tsali and his family were captured along with others in the mountains of North Carolina by federal soldiers. They were to be removed to the *darkening West.* One of the soldiers poked Tsali's wife with a bayonet, to make her speed up. Tsali and his kinsmen jumped the soldiers and killed at least one while the others escaped. The Cherokee ran away, deep into the mountains to join others who had hidden there to survive on roots, wild game, and fruit till the dark times became a thing of the past. General Winfield Scott, in charge of the removal, agreed to let the others stay free in the mountains if Tsali and his kinsmen would turn themselves in. Tsali agreed to the sacrifice. He, his brother, and two oldest sons were shot to death.

Some four hundred Cherokee had bought land in North Carolina outside the Cherokee Nation and were not obligated to be removed to Indian Territory. These Indians, along with those who hid in the mountains, grew into what is today the Eastern Band of Cherokee in and around the Qualla Reservation.

Night falls as I get within five miles of Current River in Van Buren. I'm too excited to camp though. Dogs bark as I walk through the dark and catch glimpses of families seated in houses flickering by the light of TVs. From time to time, someone within a house will walk across the room and cast a shadow as if he were only an illusion between commercials. I like being a ghost in the night who peeks at America, and it doesn't cost a single thin dime.

Van Buren, little more than a village, twinkles in the near

distance as I come around the curve to hear the roar of Current River, foaming white in the moonlight. A massive old bridge, as long as a football field, leads into town. I start across it and a truck rumbles toward me with such weight and power that the old steel bridge begins to shake as if an earthquake is at hand. I grab the railing, freezing with frost, till the truck passes. Then I find myself staring down some five or six stories into the misty cold river. A single light looms out of nowhere downstream and starts my way as a small motor, with its constant tiny explosions, attacks the beauty of the night.

I step from the bridge into Van Buren, as quiet as a hill. I like it this way, for it seems all mine. It's so late I'd rather get a room than pitch my tent in the cold. But money is running low and I go down to the river under the bridge to camp. In my great wisdom, I manage to pick the hardest plot of ground this side of the Mississippi.

When the boat passes with its spotlight, I curl up in my sleeping bag. Damn hard ground. I consider moving the tent, but I don't want to dress: I'm just plain old beat. I find solace in the sound of the river, rushing over rocks, till I hear danger: Someone is walking my way. I peek out the tent, but the coast is clear. I lie down again and pull the sleeping bag around my head only to hear the footsteps again. Now, for the first time on my journey, I pull my knife and open its surgical steel blade. I hate to perform an operation this late at night, and only with moonlight, but if I have to, I will. I open the tent and ease my head outside. I hold the knife like the New York street fighter I'm not. Once again, I see no one. I lie back down—my knife ready—and pull the sleeping bag around my head. Yes, this time the footsteps are louder, *closer.* I don't move, and they come *closer* and faster and *faster* till I discover the intruder is in my tent: It's *me.* My eyelashes brushing against the nylon sleeping bag create a sound like footsteps. Some warrior I am.

Every time a truck passes in the night, the old bridge creaks and rattles. I develop a new compassion for trolls and wake at dawn feeling like I've been tied at the stake and stoned with tomatoes. I'm dirty, my clothes are wrinkled, and I need to shave. No wonder the waitress at Floating River Restaurant looks at me as if I've just popped in for a quick coffee between battles.

I get a room at the Hawthorne Motel and a shower and clean clothes transform me into a human being, or something close to it. I don't want to sleep now, but I turn back the covers just to run my fingers over clean soft sheets. Oh, won't tonight be warm and cozy. Then it hits me how the Cherokee had only torn and soiled blankets when they passed through this area. This thought doesn't burden me with guilt. It makes me realize, once again, how easy my life is. How rich I am.

The frost has long ago melted when I go outside to hang my hand-washed clothes on the wire fence around the swimming pool, which is collecting red and yellow leaves. They sail about in ripples as a cool breeze lifts mist from the nearby Current River. I head for the bridge, but I get detoured into an old two-story house with a sign promising junk and antiques.

I fall instantly in love with Bunny when I discover her sitting atop an armoire in a dusty room at the bottom of a staircase leading to the owner's living quarters. Bunny, a dog, was carved from wood some sixty or seventy years ago to sit and look so much like the RCA dog that I expect to hear music begin at any moment. She sits on a board with an empty bowl at her feet and her name is written on it as if by a child or an old man. Some of the black and white paint is chipping off, but where else can a man buy a folk art friend for twelve bucks? I'm guessing that Bunny was the family dog of whoever carved her with such loving care. I don't understand the world I live in, for who could junk such a work of the heart?

I carry Bunny in a paper bag down to the bridge to show her where I slept last night. She's the best listener in the whole wide world. She clings to every word and never blinks an eye in protest. I can do no wrong. Trouble is, I can do no right either. Come on, Bunny, how about a wag of the tail, a wet tongue, a whine, or even a growl. Anything to let me know you can feel. No, she won't budge a hair from her eternal gaze over the empty bowl. It's okay. I love her still. She has her ways and I have mine.

Yes, Bunny and I are having the thrill of a lifetime as we stand on the rusty bridge over Current River. Her with a wooden heart, and me still in a fever over Venda. Ah, her lips. To passing motorists I must look like a man with a dog in a bag who's about to jump to the water below. Then it hits me: Why don't I phone Venda to see if she wants to drive to Van Buren tomorrow? But on the other hand, won't it hurt like hell, if she does come, to get closer and have to part again? It wouldn't be fair to her or me. But enough of this boring logic; I follow my emotions and head for the phone like a man with a mission. Hurry, Bunny.

# CHAPTER TWENTY-THREE

VENDA ARRIVES THE next morning with her five-year-old son, Velven. My night was charged with erotic dreams and I had hoped she would come alone.

I brought you something, she says.

Well, I say, I don't know if he'll hold up on the Trail. Won't you miss him?

Not him, she laughs. *This*.

She pulls a piece of leather, almost as big as my shirt, from the car. It's painted and burned with two Indians, feathers dangling from their long hair.

I did it after you called, she says.

I hug her and it feels even better than it did four days ago. Velven gives a challenging eye.

I want my trucks, Mama, he says.

So it is. Boys and men are forever wanting something from women. I release her and she takes two toy trucks from the car. Sorry, she whispers. I didn't *want* to let go.


The largest spring in America, Big Spring, is only five miles south of Van Buren, and we drive there as the day warms and leaves drift to the ground. Except for ocean waves crashing against cliffs, I've never seen such aquatic beauty. The spring bubbles from a cave into a turquoise pool with such force that I'm convinced the earth is alive. Its heart, as big as the moon, must beat at its molten core. It's easy to see why the Indians considered the spot sacred.

A sign says DO NOT ENTER near the mouth of the spring. But it seems a shame to be so close to the source and not touch it. We cross the barrier chain and stick our hands into the water as it shoots from the earth into the pool. In her eyes I see an equal passion. I can't deny that it scares me as much as it excites me. I fight myself; I can't afford to fall in love. This is just a break from the walk, I tell myself. I have too far to go to let it become anything else.

A small cave opens near the spring and to enter we must squat like ducks. Velven, on the other hand, is short enough to walk right in as if he owns this little kingdom.

Can you teach me that trick? I say.

He smiles and walks around me just to rub it in.

No, he says. I *won't* show you.

I grab him and pull him into my arms as I lean back against the rock wall. Venda sits beside me and I hang on to Velven as he tries to escape. I begin to tickle his ribs and his laughter echoes from the cave onto the bubbling spring as if none of us has a care in the world. I believe in a place in the human soul that opens only at special moments to collect memories like kings collect diamonds and rubies. This is one of those moments when I stack my riches.

We spread a blanket on the grass in a field and Venda plays her guitar and sings: *Some say love, it is a razor* . . .

Venda puts so much of herself in the song, however, that I begin to forget the words and simply listen to her voice. I also watch her lips as they part. We still haven't kissed and her tongue entices me as much as the pain and suffering in her eyes remind me that I am not alone with my scars.

Velven is playing in a swing and when she finishes the song, I ease the guitar to the grass and put my arms around her. Her legs are longer than mine but they fit into my thighs as easily as her lips meet mine. At first, the kiss is so tender it barely goes beyond the weight of breath. Then the tip of my tongue traces her moist lips to make sure it's time to move ahead. She responds with faint moans as her mouth opens to pull my tongue into her warm wetness. As our confidence grows our bodies press tighter into each other as if to make certain we don't escape. Once our tongues entwine we head for the stars. I haven't been to this altitude in so long, I had almost forgotten that man *can* fly. Oh, and what a contrast to walking the Trail of Tears. I never want to come down again. This is the way to feel every day. My hand now finds its way under her blouse in the back, to touch skin as smooth as her lips. My thumb runs along the muscles of her spine toward her neck, only to become fingers going in the opposite direction to dare down a couple of inches into her jeans, where the curve of her hips make me lose any trace of sanity that got this far. My tongue begins to explore her neck, where the song came from, when I discover Velven coming toward us with less than a smile.

I don't want to swing anymore, he says. I'm hungry.

So, back to earth Venda and I come. We pack the blanket and guitar into the car and drive into Van Buren. We grab a bite in a café. Video games, only a few feet away, drill us with eerie electronic beeps, whistles, and explosions. One game allows the player to kill a cop or outrun him, while a second game gives him the power to make a coke bust with a submachine gun.

Listen to it, I say. The world trying to shoot a hole in our day.

I hate those machines, she says.

Can I play, Mama? says Velven.

No, she says. You'll get enough of that when you're older.

I don't understand how the day gets gone so quickly, but the sun begins to set. Venda's head is hurting and it makes it all the harder to say good-bye. I hate the thought of her driving in pain for two hours through the dark to get back home. We go to the bridge so Velven can feel it shake. When a truck finally comes, he grabs the steel railing.

Will it fall? he says.

No, I say. It just feels that way.

Venda and I put our arms around each other till the earthquake passes. When the truck is gone and the bridge is stable again, she begins to cry.

It's okay, Mama, says Velven. We're safe now.

I watch them drive away as dusk comes and walk back to the bridge. I stand here till dark and study Current River roaring into the night. When I begin to chill I return to my room at the Hawthorne Motel. Bunny greets me with her sad wooden eyes.

What do I do with these feelings? I say to her.

*   *   *

The next day I wrap Bunny in the leather painted with two Indians and place them in a box. I mail them to Alabama and hit the Trail.

I've always been intrigued with scars because they show that something happened to someone, and especially in today's world of hype, glamour, and cosmetic surgery—to hide or disguise what's genuine in people—scars fascinate me all the more. They promise that their owners are part of the human experience. Venda had a scar four or five inches long under her forearm where she cut it on a rock when, as a child, she fell while chasing a bull. I have a scar of equal length on my right leg. I got it from a fall when four dogs chased me in the woods. I deserved the cut because some other boys and myself had been throwing rocks at them. Today, five miles north of Van Buren, I'm attacked by a Doberman pinscher.

The dog charges toward me with such speed, it's as if it had been coiled and waiting for me at the side of the house. As it growls and runs, its teeth promise hell. I don't have time to see a stick, let alone grab it, for protection. I unsnap the pack belt and slide from the shoulder strap only a split second before those teeth get within inches of my leg. I hold the pack as a guard between me and the dog as I consider kicking its head down its throat. Finally, the owner runs from the house and pulls him away. I have enough adrenaline in my blood to revive a heart attack patient.

Today isn't my day. I walk five more miles and spot another Doberman. I pray that he's chained, but forget it. When he spots me, he begins to strut in front of the weathered farmhouse on a hill. I look around for a stick, but there's nothing. I'm surrounded by fields for a mile each way. I'm tempted to stop and thumb a ride for a couple of miles, but this crazy thing called pride puts a stop to that, pronto. I keep walking and looking straight ahead as if he'll vanish into thin air or something. When I do turn his way, I spot a *second* Doberman. They now walk side by side as if trained to attack as a team. I consider shouting at the farmhouse that I like my flesh just the way it is, thank you. I don't need more scars for personality. But I decide against calling for help because it might trigger the two dogs to attack. I could maybe keep *one* off me with the pack, but not two.

The two dogs now disappear behind the barn and I think it's too good to be true. I'm right, for they reappear with a *third* Doberman. I eye the farmhouse, but no one appears. I'm plain old scared to the bone as the three dogs begin to study me like prey. I consider running, but it would only throw gasoline on the fire. Up ahead is a telephone pole. If they attack, I can climb it and hang there like a damn monkey till someone comes to help. I'm not into the macho image so much, but the vision of clinging to the pole disgusts me.

My luck may be changing when I discover a post lying beside the fence. It's longer than a baseball bat and twice as thick. I pick it up and the dogs come closer. I don't want to hurt one of them, but I sure don't want their teeth in my throat. To hell with climbing the telephone pole. If they attack, I'll break their backs. Or try to.

I'm some fifty yards past the barn when I turn back to see them still watching. I carry the pole till I round the next curve. I was scared of the dogs, but something else frightened me much more: The part of me that *wanted* them to attack. I throw the post as far into the woods as I can, as if trying to free myself of that instinct. I'm relieved when a blue jay flies across the Trail to offer its lifting squawk of a whistle.

# CHAPTER TWENTY-FOUR

THAT AFTERNOON I enter the Mark Twain National Forest and camp beside a creek. I'm miles from any houses, or dogs, and this suits me just fine.

It's three hours till dark and I walk along the creek in hopes of finding some arrowheads or other Indian relics. I don't find any chips of flint to suggest that this was an ancient campsite, but the water excites me with some small bass.

I dig into my pack and pull out a fish hook, a float, and some line. I break a limb from a fallen tree and use it as a fishing pole. When I find a worm under a rock, I'm in business. I throw the bait into the deepest pool and sit on the ground to await my trophy catch. An hour passes and I don't even get a bite. Unless I count the mosquito that got me on the arm.

A sweet sadness sets in as I begin to think about Venda and

what a great day we had yesterday. I place my pole in a Y-shaped branch stuck in the ground and wander upstream to get my mind on something else. A squirrel, sitting on a limb, begins to bark as I step across a rotten log covered with moss. Its busy tail jerks with each bark and I bark back. It runs up the tree and disappears on the other side. As silly as it seems, I wish now that I hadn't mailed Bunny back home. Wooden and mute as she is, I wish she were making the walk with me.

I come to a shallow place in the creek. I take off my shoes and socks and go down to the water. I stick my right foot in the stream and it's so cold that I jerk it right out again. But my feet are a little swollen and I force myself to wade up to my calves to soothe them. In a couple of minutes I don't mind the icy water at all. I like this ancient ritual of going to water. I wash my face and arms as a yellow poplar leaf drifts into the stream to float away.

I turn over a couple of rocks in the creek in hopes of locating a crawfish. It's not until the fifth rock that I find one about the size of my thumb. Its powerful tail propels it backward, while its pincers stand ready to take on the world. I keep it busy with my left hand while my right one catches it between my thumb and index finger. I lift it from the water and hold it against the sky, its hair-thin feelers dangling in the breeze. The Cherokee would cut the meat from the tail and put it on their skin, blistered from poison ivy. I consider using the meat for fish bait, but I don't. I lower the crawfish into the water and release it. It shoots backward into deeper water to disappear into a blue-green pool. For a few seconds, it strikes me as odd that I'm probably the first and only human being it will ever see. In fact, I'm starting to think this way more and more as I walk across the country. For example, when the yellow poplar leaf dropped from the tree a few minutes ago, it struck me how that will never happen again with that particular leaf. I saw it at that one rare moment when it was released from its source. It's easy to say that such a small thing means absolutely nothing. I'm sure there are those who can take it a step further and say that anyone who spends much time thinking about such things is a fool. Well, maybe so. But the farther I walk and sleep beneath the stars the quicker I'm coming to the conclusion that a man who doesn't spend enough time thinking about how precious and intricate life is has no wisdom at all.

On the way back to my camp, I find a wild-turkey feather sticking from pine needles. It's the first I've seen on the Trail and I stick it in my hat next to the crow feather and a blue jay feather I found before I got to Van Buren. Yes, the hat's coming alive now. Why, by the end of the journey it might be able to hum a tune. I wear the feathers in my hat because I love birds, their songs and flights. I wear the snake rattler because it crawls on the earth. I think that's man in a thumbnail. He spends most of his time crawling, when he wants to soar. Thank goodness his spirit sometimes does.

I get a thrill when I return to camp to find my fishing line pulled tight. The pole is jerking and the red float bobs up and down. A part of me wants to grab the pole as quick as lightning while another part of me wants just to stand and watch as antici-pation builds to see what I've caught. I end up compromising and slowly bend over to reach the pole. My day is made when I pull a bass from the water. It doesn't weigh a full pound, but it's plenty big enough for tonight's dinner.

When the fire is built, I clean the fish and wash it in the creek. The Cherokee sometimes caught fish by damming up a stream and lacing it with walnut hulls, forcing the numbed fish to float to the top. My father caught fish this way when he was only a boy growing up on Sand Mountain. In the night, he and others also caught birds by putting a torch, made from a lighted pine knot, to bushes. The confused birds would fly, only to be knocked down by giant hands made of dogwood branches. My father and his friends would roast the birds over an open fire by the creek and eat them like his ancestors did hundreds of years ago.

I wrap the cleaned bass in aluminum foil and place it near the coals to bake. I have always been awed by fire. Nothing excited me more when I was a kid than to throw spears, shoot arrows, and build a fire in the woods. It was a secret power and a bit dangerous, and forbidden because it could destroy. It offered light and warmth, but it had no mercy and would burn clothes and skin as quickly as it burned leaves or sticks. I learned to respect it as soon as I could touch it. Like feelings, spirits, and ghosts, it was something that couldn't be seen all the time, but it was watching and waiting for just the right spark to come alive and shake man out of his arrogance, whether it came from a bolt of lightning striking a tree or the *Challenger* exploding into a giant flaming ball.

As night falls the fire makes me feel needed. Stick by stick, I keep it alive. It bonds me not only with my ancestors, but with the Earth and heavens. The sun is stored in the wood I now burn and the moon, over the trees, reflects sunlight from the Earth. As I take the fish from the fire I feel at one with the Great Mystery. For the moment, I have no fear of dying and returning to It.

When I do die, I don't want to be embalmed and put in a vault. I want simply to be placed in a hole and covered with earth. I want to feed the trees where owls hoot and crows squawk their hearts out. Yes, of course, I'd rather live forever, but since I can't I might as well try to make the leap with a touch of grace. For all I can prove, that yellow poplar leaf that floated down the creek earlier was a distant cousin once buried where I now sit.

But on to something I'm sure of: The foil, wrapped around

the bass, is hot as hell as I open it to get to dinner. I have no salt or pepper, but it doesn't matter. The meat is tender and delicious as I use my fingers to eat it. When I'm finished, I hold the bones against the moon just to see a new shape in the night and recall once again how everything is connected. The moon controls the ocean tides, where billions of fish this very moment are born and die. Also, where I sit was once covered by the sea. It's not every day that I'm excited by my own insignificance.

The Earth's forests are being destroyed an acre per second and our oxygen supply is slowly vanishing. I've never been a fan of choking to death and if I think about our environment too much I become not only sad but outraged.

Tonight, however, here in the woods with the fire flickering and the creek bubbling, I give in to the illusion that all is safe and sound in America and across the globe. Except for the possibility of bears, I fear nothing. Call it God or the Great Spirit or whatever, I feel protected. If the walk ends right now, it is a success. In this Modern World which goes a thousand miles per hour, I'm finally catching up with myself. I might even decide to stay with me.

The fire fades and I crawl into the tent. The earth beneath is so soft with leaves that a real bed couldn't be better. The moon is bright and when I hear a splash, I look out to see a raccoon at the creek. It either sees me or gets my scent, for it vanishes into the woods as if the ground itself opens up to swallow it.

My pack is by my side and my hat sits atop it. The feathers stick from it and seem to reach among the stars. If I could feel like this all the time I could be a holy man. Free of the world and all its troubles, I fall into the great and glorious kingdom of sleep.

\*   \*   \*

It's close to impossible for a man to spend three days in the Mark Twain National Forest and not get closer to himself as well as Nature. But it's also equally difficult not to long for human contact.

I welcome that contact, when peaceful, in any human shape or form. In the Ozark Tavern it presents itself as two pool players, Fat Indian—a fishhook in his hat—and Two Dudes—so nicknamed because of his size—who insist on buying me one beer after another, along with the barmaid and Chicago Tony, who slips my pack on his back and parades about the tavern with an aging limp.

Look at me, everybody, he says. I'm walking back to Chicago.

Good, says Two Dudes, racking the balls. I'll open the door for you.


In Marble Hill, that contact comes in the form of a country doctor, John Inglehart, and his wife, Jean. They invite me to their home for lunch. It's Sunday and the chicken is so good, it makes me just a little homesick for Alabama.

I *could* go to a city, says Dr. John, and make some real money. But I feel needed here in the country. Especially the old folks like it when I make house calls. I'm not saying I don't miss the money. I wrestle with myself about it every day. But, no, I couldn't live in a city and look myself in the eye. It's a calling to be here.

With my gut filled with chicken, potatoes, salad, bread, coffee, and cake, I hit the Trail and keep walking after dark. I'm only twenty miles from the Mississippi River and my halfway point of Cape Girardeau, and I'm too excited to sleep.

# CHAPTER TWENTY-FIVE

A T THE INTERSECTION of Highways 34 and 72, I find an all-night convenience store and enter to buy some orange juice and sit a spell. Garrett, the cashier, gives me a cool shoulder when I ask if he can cash a U.S. postal money order.

I'm not allowed to, he says.

I find enough change, however, to buy the juice and take a seat over by the microwave next to the nacho dip. Yep, I'm back in the lap of civilization again. Regular, Unleaded, and Super Unleaded—just take your pick. Don't forget that discount when you pay cash.

Garrett, only nineteen, begins to warm as we talk. He's tall, handsome, and just vulnerable enough to make his eyes interesting. He's in his first year of college.

I share a house, he says, with two other guys. I never lived

away from home before. It's all I can do to pay my bills and get
my homework done. I don't know if I'll make it or not.

You'll make it, I say.

I hope you're right, he says. I'm studying music. I like to mix
blues with classical. My teachers don't get it. They want me to be
pure. But I *need* to play the blues sometimes. It's the only way I
can deal with sadness and anger.

It becomes clearer why I like Garrett so much. He lives on a
feeling plane. I've just met him, but already I'm wondering what
will become of him. Will his music take him deeper into himself,
from where he can lift the world from its own blues, or will he
end up married with two kids to work at a job he hates while the
guitar becomes a relic in the closet?

I'm trying to learn how to read music, Garrett continues. I
learned to play from an old black man. He sat in one room while
I sat in another. He'd hit a note and make me identify it. I got
good ears. I'd play the note back to him.

I check behind the store for a place to pitch my tent. But the
ground is too rocky and I head on down the Trail with a flashlight
in my hand. Garrett told me of a church only a mile down the
road where I might camp, but it has a house on either side and I
don't want company this late at night. I finally find an inviting
spot in an apple orchard next to a Coca-Cola billboard promising, IT'S THE REAL THING. I'm sure the Indians who passed here 150
years ago would see the humor. I'm not so sure about how loud
they'd laugh.

I go through enough red tape to short-circuit a paper shred-
der at Southeast Missouri State University, in Cape Girardeau, to
get a room for six bucks, but it's worth it. I can dream I'm back in
college as I climb a hill across campus to find my bed.

It's nothing short of heaven to drop my pack in the six-dollar room and take a shower. My body aches more now than any time on the walk. It's as though some of the pain has been holding off till I reached the halfway point, to jump out and tackle me. I collapse on the bed as if discovering the greatest invention since sight.

I can't say that I awake two hours later refreshed enough to jump out of bed, but I'm at least back in one piece and eager to see the Mississippi and its riverfront town. After a month on the Trail it now seems a bit odd to be free of my pack. I also leave my hat behind as I walk into town. Without them, I feel just a bit naked and this concerns me. I don't want to depend on them for identity any more than I do on a certain kind of car. When you really get through all the ego bullshit, don't we want to stand naked with the beauty of our bodies, the knowledge of our minds, and the freedom of our spirits? Okay, so you don't agree. You want the new car. Fine, just don't run over me and I won't stand naked in front of you.

Some of the Cape's buildings are over two hundred years old with wrought iron balconies. That spots in the plastered walls are crumbling onto the streets and sidewalks only adds to the atmosphere. It also gives me a chance to play plaster polo and kick the crumbling chunks to the side as I approach a bar, overlooking Long Man, the river god. The Mississippi twists, turns, and boils as if a monster lives on its bottom. That monster, said the old Cherokee, was called *Uktena*.

Uktena was a man who turned into a snake as big as a tree and was sent to kill the sun when it tried to burn the Indians on Earth. But Uktena failed and became outraged. If a man even looked at it, his family would die. The Cherokee were so afraid of Uktena that they had it sent up to *Galun'lati* to join other such forces. Others like it still live on Earth, however, and horns stick from their mighty armored heads. In their foreheads ride blazing diamonds while their scaled bodies send sparks flying. They hide, this very second, in high mountains and deep rivers.

As I study the roaring Mississippi with this myth on my mind a chill eases up my arms and down my back. I don't actually believe that a giant snake lives down there, but I better understand why the Indians were afraid to travel to Indian Territory by boat, as some of them did. It's here, right before me, that they crossed Long Man on flatboats. They also crossed ten miles north of here where a Trail of Tears park has been built.

The next day I go to that park to see where the daughter of Jesse Bushyhead is buried. That name sounds familiar because he founded the Old Baptist Mission Church where I camped the second night of the walk and met Hank and his dog, Red. The park is beautiful, but I could spit when I see the grave, because it's covered with concrete as if it's a parking lot for toy cars. I can see Jesse Bushyhead on the Trail when his daughter died:

> I would like to gather some rocks and place them on her grave, he says, to honor her place in the earth.
>
> We don't have time, says the army captain. I'll put in a request for some concrete. Or would you prefer asphalt?

Actually, I suppose many of the soldiers who moved the Indians had heavy hearts and nightmares from seeing all the pain and suffering. John G. Burnett was in the U.S. Cavalry and helped remove the Cherokee. When he turned eighty in 1890, he wrote the following letter to his grandchildren.

The removal of the Cherokee Indians from their lifelong homes in the year 1838 found me a young man in the prime of life and a soldier in the American army. Being acquainted with many of the Indians and able fluently to speak their language, I was sent as interpreter into the Smokey Mountain Country in May 1838, and witnessed the execution of the most brutal order in the history of the American warfare. I saw the helpless Cherokees arrested and dragged from their homes, driven at the bayonet point into the stockades. And in the chill of drizzling rain on an October morning I saw them loaded like cattle or sheep into six hundred and forty wagons and started toward the west.

One can never forget the sadness and solemnity of that morning. Chief John Ross led in prayer, and when the bugle sounded and the wagons started rolling many of the children rose to their feet and waved their little hands good-bye to their mountain homes, knowing they were leaving forever. Many of these helpless people did not have blankets and many of them had been driven from home barefooted . . .

The room at the university is booked for tonight, so I get lodging at the Olive Branch, the Cape's only bed and breakfast. The owners' cat, Dylan—named after both Bob and Thomas— makes me realize how much I miss my cat, Rosco. Indeed, *home* is starting to hit me more and more each day.

I walk down to scout the great bridge over the Mississippi

and get my spirits dampened because there's no walkway. I can't
chance walking the bridge, either, for it's much too narrow. I'd
just be asking for a car or truck to turn me into deviled ham or a
lump in the river—going once, twice—so long, sucker. Hey, look
how the hat with the feathers floats.

I don't want to thumb across the bridge, but I don't know
what else to do. On a long shot, however, I call the police station
to see if anyone can give me an escort across the river. I prepare
myself for the brush-off.

Sure, says the officer. What time do you want to cross?

I hang up the phone and I'm glad no one can see me as my
eyes become misty. Americans *do* care. This *is* a great country.

A TV crew awaits me at the bridge as a cop on a motorcycle
turns on his twirling red light and motions for me to walk in front
of him. The traffic begins to back up and I decide to *run* across
the bridge. Okay, okay, a bit dramatic, but this is my first police
escort. I'm not used to such official attention.

The traffic facing me is, of course, still moving. Halfway
across the bridge it dawns on me how this must look to the
drivers. I'm running and a motorcycle cop is chasing me.

With fifty pounds on my back my legs begin to tire and my
lungs burn. I mean *burn.* I want to forget this running jazz and
walk the rest of the way. But now a line of traffic a half mile long
is watching and I can't lose face. I finally make it to the other
side.

My heroes have never been cops, but this one on the motorcycle seems like a good guy inside the dark sunglasses and hel-
met. I thank him and when we shake hands, I recall the Amish I
met driving his buggy. I also envision a student back in Springfield, at Evangel College, who asked if he could hold my hand
while he prayed to ask for my safe journey and that what I'm
doing would make a difference in the world. I've never had a

stranger do this before. I agreed to the prayer to please him. I rationalized that it was research; I'd simply observe like an anthropologist. But when his hand gripped mine and he asked God for help, I melted into the moment that two men could touch as brothers and seek the highest power. So now, as I grip the hand of the cop, I also grip the men I met before, as if an invisible chain is being built to stretch from Oklahoma to Alabama. Of course, I don't mention this to the cop. He may not be into chains.

Now that I'm in Illinois I'm in the heartland of America, and soybean fields stretch for miles along the Mississippi River. This is also a flyway for geese, charging the sky just above the treetops with honking Vs. I haven't hunted in years because I haven't liked the idea of killing any living creature. But I now find myself aiming an imaginary bow and arrow at an extra-fat goose as it glides over. I'd like to roast it over a campfire in the night. I'd save the feathers to add to gourd masks when I return home.

The Cherokee made masks from large gourds and cut holes in them for the eyes, nose, and mouth. I've made several myself, and they hang outside my cabin, brightly dyed red and yellow, with dried seeds as decoration.

I've walked twenty miles since I crossed the Mississippi. The café, where I stand, closed twenty minutes ago. I must look like Bunny, peering over her empty bowl, as I stare through the window at the menu. No, you can't be closed. There's a mistake here. I'm hungry. Hungry. Do you hear, *hungry*? But it's a useless cry. No one lingers to wash dishes or mop the floor. The CLOSED sign speaks only the truth.

I check my map. I've had better news. It's ten miles, three fun-filled hours by foot, to the next town.

# CHAPTER TWENTY-SIX

THE SUNSET, THE prettiest I've seen so far on the walk, casts its promise of night as I reach Dutch Creek, where the Cherokee camped for weeks, waiting for the Mississippi River to thaw. Hundreds died here, where a picnic table now sits, and even their shallow graves are unmarked. I open my pack and find the rose Lewis Day gave me back in Arkansas. I take a couple of the dried petals and squat by the stream. I drop them into the water for those who died here. They drift downstream and disappear into the bend's shadows.

When the Cherokee crossed the Mississippi, they either traveled to Indian Territory via Springfield, the way I came, or they cut south from Cape Girardeau toward Batesville, Arkansas, before heading west again. By the thirteen groups splitting up that way, they may have had a better chance of finding more wild game to kill to feed themselves. They also may have hoped to slow the spread of various diseases by isolating those who were already infected.

I've given up on eating tonight. It's another five miles to the next town and I'm just too tired to keep going. I would camp here on Dutch Creek, but it's so close to the road, my tent would be an easy target for rocks or beer bottles.

I move on, hoping to find a good spot as soon as possible when the new moon appears. I love the moon and all its magic, except for this phase because it always takes me back to the night of my greatest horror: When I was married and living in Oklahoma City, I was a community librarian. It was a fun place to work and I had the freedom, till the conversations got too real to suit my boss, to have a discussion group for high school kids. My favorite was Brenda, who was fifteen. We became friends and over the years I saw her become a woman. When I was divorced, she became my lover. A while later, against my advice, she left college to come to New Orleans where I lived. She wanted to experience life and took a job as a waitress in the Hilton Hotel, overlooking the Mississippi River. I went on a trip for three weeks and she stayed in my apartment while I was away. The night I returned to Alabama from Colorado, she quit her job and was thrilled at going home to Oklahoma for a few days before meeting me in Alabama. That night I began to sense or imagine that evil —a great evil—was after her. I wanted to call her, but she had no phone. From my trip I had gathered a whale's tooth, a candle holder, and a leather bullet pouch. I had placed them by my bed on a table when I unpacked and I got the strongest urge to move them. I believed that, not unlike some voodoo in New Orleans, they were casting a spell. I had the power to alter that spell—of evil—if I would only do so. I had never had such a feeling in my life and I refused to listen to a tired brain which had been on the road for three weeks. I went to bed and awoke two hours later in a horrible sweat as the phone rang. I answered it, and it was Brenda's father calling from Oklahoma City. He had just gotten a call from New Orleans. Brenda, walking to the store, had been shot in the back by a kid for no apparent reason. The bullet was lodged in her spine. It paralyzed her from the waist down. Who shot her and why is still a mystery.

She wore my shirt when she was shot. Sometimes I can still see the bullet hole staring out at me. I leave it up to those who like to argue facts and fantasies as to how I gathered that something horrible was about to happen to her. I only know two things. First, I now listen to my inner voice. There is a spirit world of some nature as real as man's world. Second, my best friend will never walk again and the moon in its new phase, like it is tonight, drips blood down to earth and onto the Trail of Tears. This story is part of what I was feeling and thinking back in Tahlequah when the little redheaded girl stood in the café booth with her finger pointed at me to practice sorcery. I simply didn't have the nerve to talk about it then.

Dutch Creek disappears into the twilight as a van pulls over behind me; its lights shine in my eyes. I've been offered no less than thirty or forty rides since I left Tahlequah and I assume this is another such gesture of kindness.

I walk toward the van to say, Thanks, but no thanks, when the door is opened by Hank. Red, his Irish setter, sticks his head out too.

How? says Hank, raising his hand like a TV Indian.

By foot and luck. I smile. How are you?

A helluva lot better than the last time I saw you, he says. You've come a couple of miles yourself.

I load my pack into the van and we travel back toward Cape

Girardeau to a roadside park near the Mississippi River. I build a fire and set up my tent while Hank drives on into town to get some beer and a couple of steaks. Now that I have company, the moon above doesn't seem so cold and cruel. Rather, I view it as actually having a personality. Tonight it's mostly dark, but who doesn't range between that and light?

These aren't as good as the steaks back in Texas, says Hank, placing the meat on the grill. But I got the best ones I could find. Mind if I doctor 'em up Mexican style, or do you like 'em on the gringo side?

You're the doctor, I say.

He gets some dried chilies from his van and rubs them into the steaks. Once they're placed on the grill, we sit in the grass and guzzle a couple of beers. When Red sniffs the meat, Hank throws one of the empty cans at him.

You know better than that, shouts Hank. Damn, I hate for him to look at me like that. Come here. Come on, boy. I'm sorry, he adds, rubbing the dog's neck. Besides, I think there was some beer left in that can. I'd better turn the steaks.

I'll get 'em, I say.

The fire has burned down to only coals, and though I rarely eat red meat, I love the smell of the steaks cooking under the stars. But it's not just that, it's the company that makes 'em seem so appetizing. I assumed that Hank had simply become another face I'd never see again. Bunny, with all her stoic beauty, doesn't really compare to Red, who can run and jump and place his head in your lap to make you feel like you're the master of the universe.

Your mother okay? I say, taking another beer from the bag as I join Hank back on the grass.

Yeah, says Hank. She's doing fine now. She had a block near the heart, but they did that balloon surgery on her. She's as mean as ever again. When I left this morning, she was pounding a fence post into the ground like nobody's business. It was a real screwy month. Me and my two brothers got a lot of shit talked about that had built up over the years. Damn shame it took Mother almost dying to get us to that point, but things are pretty good right now. I feel better about myself. I was feeling like I had failed, since my brothers have families and good jobs and all that, but a lot of that was just stuff in my head. I think they even envy me a little. Anyway, we got the air cleared. I told my mother I loved her too. I'd never done that before. Look what she gave me.

He hands me his car keys and on the ring is a medal. A car passes and I hold it up in the light for a better look, but I still don't recognize it.

It's a Purple Heart, says Hank. My father got it in World War Two. He left us when I was a kid, but I'm glad to get it. I'm thinking about trying to find him. He was a heavy boozer and may be dead by now, but if he's not, I'd like to know more about him. Doesn't make a lot of sense, does it?

It makes all the sense in the world, I say. I've thought a lot about the Indians who died on the Trail. How it must've felt to sons and daughters to leave a parent buried in the woods without even a marker. Yeah, wanting to find your father makes a lot of sense.

I cut into my steak and it's spicy-hot enough to make my eyes water when I begin chewing. A piece of French bread tones it down, however, and I like my stomach full again.

You remember I told you, says Hank, about my coke-head girlfriend who ripped me off and got the hell out of Dodge?

Yeah, I say. She drew Mick Jagger on one of your sweat-shirts.

That's her, says Hank, slipping a piece of meat into Red's mouth. Well, she phoned me down in Texas. Apologized and wants to see me again. I don't know what to do. I'm confused. She said she'll go into a treatment program, but I know the odds of her staying straight are less than a snowball staying frozen in hell. Why do so many people with good hearts have screwed up minds?

You have a delicate situation on your hands, I say. I guess it all depends on how much you love her. Or need her.

I need *some* woman, he sighs. I don't like that about myself, but it's true. I just get too lonely otherwise. I hate the whole bar scene. I'm getting too old for all the bullshit anyway. I just want somebody to love and trust. The world's a pretty damn spooky place these days. You had much trouble?

No, I say. People have been great. I've been lucky.

It's not luck, he says, opening another beer. You got the gods on your side. What you're doing has meaning.

I really wonder, I say. It means a lot to me. And I see that it's touching a lot of people. But am I just a distraction for a while because their lives are so routine, or will the walk make them want to follow their own dreams as well as think about humanity? I really don't know.

Sure, it matters, he says. I thought a lot about what you're doing. Maybe a little crazy, but the world needs more of that kind of crazy. Look at all the TV and newspaper attention you're getting. You're just one person. What if a thousand, no, a million, *hell, five million* people walked across America to Washington to get the politicians to clean up our environment? Yeah, man, there's been nothing like that in history.

You sound like a die-hard hippie, I laugh.

I'm a little high, he says, sipping his beer. But I'm not drunk. It could happen. Anything can happen if we really want it to. People just got to work together.

Know what this reminds me of? I say, running my fingers through Red's thick hair.

What?

That scene from *Easy Rider,* I say. They're sitting around the fire and Jack Nicholson's character is talking about how there's really flying saucers, but the aliens won't present themselves because our antiquated society isn't ready for them. They would blow a fuse.

It's true, man, says Hank. It's as true as those cars passing there on the road.

I don't sleep in my tent tonight. I simply pull out my sleeping bag and slide into it. Hank does the same only a few feet away and Red curls up between us. We talk late into the night and Hank falls asleep first. From time to time, I stroke Red and he wags his tail. Life is full.

The next morning I awake to find that Hank and his sleeping bag have vanished from their spot only a few feet away. Half asleep, I'm jolted that he would leave without saying good-bye. Not to mention that I've got to retrace some fifteen miles back to where we met last night.

But the smell of coffee rescues my doubts. Hank stands over the fire with a coffeepot in his hands. Red sniffs around a tree.

I thought you'd left, I say, crawling from the sleeping bag.

I was tempted to, in the night. He grins. You snore like a damn train. Want some coffee?

Hank scrambles some eggs with tomatoes and onions and we eat them in corn tortillas. This is the first breakfast I've had from a fire on the Trail and I can't think of a better way to start the day. But, on the other hand, if Venda were here . . .

If I didn't have a house to wire back in Chicago, says Hank, I'd be tempted to make the walk with you.

You'd be welcome, I say, thinking that he's only dreaming.

Life's too short, he says. It's just too damn short.

We feed the leftovers to Red and I load my pack into the van. Hank takes me back to where we met last night and he gets out to tell me good-bye. When our hands lock, we find ourselves embracing. A bit embarrassed about caring, our eyes are a little funny when we look at each other again.

Thanks for the meals, I say. The company wasn't too bad.

You're gonna make it, he says. You're gonna make it all the way home.

I rub Red on the head and the next thing I know I'm alone again, walking toward the Ohio River on the Kentucky border. Before I began the walk several people asked what kind of dog I was taking with me. They found it hard to believe when I said I was traveling alone. Now, for the first time, I wish someone were walking beside me. I'm sure the birds would understand.

# CHAPTER TWENTY-SEVEN

THE KNOT IN the corner of my right eye where the tick sucked has started to go down. I'm no longer anxious about some disease. But my left thigh and lower back are giving me trouble. I figure that when I ran across the bridge the pack, bouncing up and down against my lower back, knocked a vertebra out of line. It's not so painful, it's just a constant reminder that I'm flesh and bones, slowly disintegrating.

I'm reminded once again, however, just how much I have to be thankful for when I spot smoke streaming over the heads of six inmates, chopping small trees and bushes to place them on a giant fire. An armed guard stands over them and gives me a cold eye. All the men but one stop what they're doing to study me. Never in my life have I been stared at with such envy and longing. Here I am as free as a bird to walk to my heart's content, while they're chained to the island of their crimes. I can't help but think of the Cherokee who walked across the very earth where they now burn brush. They, too, were prisoners and at the mercy of armed guards. But their only crime was being different.

I think back to when the Indians were first dragged from their log houses and thrown into those thirteen stockades scattered about the old Cherokee Nation. They were held prisoners for weeks in those concentration camps, where the smell of urine and excrement was overpowering at times. Swarms of flies buzzed around their hands and faces to spread germs and bacteria by the millions. Much of their days and nights were spent chanting and praying that the Great Spirit would keep them safe from the evil witches who could bring death.

The Cherokee were no strangers to going without food, for they sometimes endured fasts before playing ball or celebrating festivals. During the time of war they often lived only on mush. But inside the stockades, even the Cherokee began to suffer from a change in diet. With what we today know about how stress weakens the immune system, it's easy to see how the Indians' bodies became vulnerable to disease and plain old heartbreak as they looked beyond the surrounding walls to where their homes once stood among the trees.

All that remains of the stockade near where I grew up in Fort Payne, Alabama, is the chimney. The last of the imprisoning logs were burned in the year I was born, 1947. Train tracks run alongside where the crumbling chimney now stands, and sometimes in the night, from my cabin high atop its hill, I hear a thunderous whistle as a train roars through the darkness, perhaps blowing about the ghosts of Cherokee like spiderwebs in the wind.

I'm both aroused and amused when one of the prison inmates shoots a fist over his head—*Power to the walker!* When the

guard steps toward him, the inmate returns to piling brush. The
lone prisoner who refuses even to raise his head continues to
work a sling blade back and forth, back and forth, in tall grass
between the road and a small lake. It's as though he's afraid to
torture himself with the daydream of walking away. Back and
forth and back and forth the blade goes, cutting his time into tiny
pieces of grass, floating in the wind and onto the lake, where
smoke drifts from the brushfire.

Only a few miles down the Trail I come to an enormous
prison, bordered not only by walls but by wire fences trimmed
with razor-sharp barbed wire. I picture men struggling every day
just to stay alive or keep from being raped. It's a nightmare come
alive.

A guard in a station wagon has apparently forgotten that free
men exist in a world beyond this glorious hell hole. He rolls
down his window and offers an expression that inspires only
contempt.

Got any ID? he snaps.

I simply take out my wallet and give him my driver's license.
I've long held to the belief that silence is the best medicine when
dealing with assholes who carry guns. Then, too, I figure if I don't
talk I won't chance interfering with him hearing himself talk,
which seems to be a big part of the power game for sad people
like him.

We don't allow hitchhiking through here, he says.

I consider walking a few steps to demonstrate my means of
transportation. But he seems to have trouble grasping this, since
I, as always, walked facing the traffic as I approached the prison.

I'm not thumbing, I say. I'm *walking*.

Uh, well, he says. It . . . you . . .

He struggles now to collect his thoughts and I reconsider my attitude. He probably hates his job and is stuck, or thinks he is, like millions of people who don't have the guts to jump ship. It *is* a prison, and I guess it's easy to imagine that I'm carrying a bomb or some such craziness in my pack to get my wayward brother or dear old dad out of the slammer.

This was an old Indian route, I say. I'm walking it to see what folks are like along it today.

I can see in his eyes that this just doesn't make any sense in today's world. I try to connect it to something he can relate to.

It's my job, I say. I'm a writer working on a book.

Who do you work for? he says, his investigative eyes drilling me with the third degree.

I free-lance, I say. No one hired me for this.

You mean you're walking for *nothing*? he says.

He copies the information from my license and returns it. Advised not to stop even to tie my shoe strings till I get several miles from the prison, I haul ass. Some people I never want to smell again.

Miles down the Trail I eat in a café. A grocery store adjoins it, and when I start to leave I'm caught by the sight of two gypsies buying a can of beans and a loaf of bread. Tripper John, as he calls himself, is in his early twenties. His red hair hangs to his waist and he wears a Pan flute around his neck on a piece of leather. His girlfriend, Sarah, is only about twenty-one and so sensual that it hurts to look at her. They carry small cloth bags over their shoulders.

You hitchhiking or walking? I say.

Hitchhiking, says Tripper John.

I'm walking, I say.

He seems to misread my interest as competition.

You walking *with* money, he says. Or *without*?

With, I say, a bit amused.

I travel without money, he says. I don't believe in it.

That must create some interesting moments, I say. How'd you get the bread and beans?

Faith, he says. Money comes to me by faith.

*I* believe in money, says Sarah. I sometimes have to pay for him.

Our last ride gave us forty bucks, says Tripper John. We've come all the way from Seattle.

You going to the gathering? she says.

I'm not sure if I am or not, I say. Which gathering are you talking about?

Rainbow Gathering, he says.

We go outside and sit on the ground. Tripper John opens the can of beans and Sarah pours them into pieces of bread to make burritos.

The Rainbow Gathering, she says, is a kind of party. It lasts for four days and starts tomorrow. It's in a field thirty miles from here. All you need is a blanket and a cup.

*Faith,* says Tripper John with bean juice dripping from his mouth, will furnish everything else.

With all this talk about faith I can't help but wonder how Venda and her people are doing back in the Ozarks high upon the hill at Zion's Order. And how about Eddy, walking to California to discover gold with his faith? Is it only a coincidence that I'm meeting so many people along the Trail who swear by faith, or am I meeting them to teach me something about what keeps a man's spirits high?

You should come to the Gathering, says Sarah. You'll meet a

lot of good people there. People trade and sell things they make, but mostly we just talk, dance, and have a good time.

Sounds like a new flower-children movement, I say.

In a way, she says, a bean falling from her bread onto the ground.

Only we won't sell out, says Tripper John. Your generation talked a good show, but they got addicted to all the candy. Comic-book dreamers, that's all they were. *I* won't sell out.

Who can say? she says. I'm taking it as it comes.

I won't sell out, he says. I'll stay free till the day I die.

I hope you do, I say. With all my heart I hope you do.

Sarah, part Cherokee, isn't aware that we now sit on the Trail of Tears. She supports herself, in part, by making jewelry, and digs into her bag to get a beautiful necklace made of shells and beads. She gives them to me for the burial ritual and Tripper John offers a tiny pouch of red dust from Pipe Rock, Montana.

This is sacred to the Indians there, he says. They make pipes from the rock. They even save the dust to spit on it and make paint. Look how pretty it is.

He sprinkles some of the red dust into his palm and spits on it. He rubs the red paint over his arm to create a streak of lightning. It transports me back to the thunderstorm where I feared for my life.

I place the necklace and the red dust in my pack, and I regret when Tripper John and Sarah finish the beans. Talking to them is like taking a time machine back twenty years. Hippies were everywhere, and rides were as easy to find as sticking out a thumb. Coffeehouses were busy with whispers of poems, free love, and idealism. I rode a chopped Harley-Davidson. I sold my bike when I got married. Free love vanished with broken hearts, getting older, and AIDS. Coffeehouses made way for computer offices. But what happened to poems and idealism? Do they huddle together on some rainy street corner, waiting for a friendly face?

We have an extra cup, says Sarah. If you want to join the Gathering.

Maybe I'll see you there, I say.

They dump their trash in a can and we walk down to the road. It hurts to leave them standing there with their thumbs out to passing cars as I walk on. A part of me wants to abandon the journey, give in to spontaneity, and get caught up in the lives of strangers at the Rainbow Gathering. Perhaps there will be a woman as free and sensual as Sarah there, without a boyfriend. Perhaps she will be wise enough to see that my cup is my whole body and spirit, aching to be filled with tenderness and passion. Then I can turn that cup over her and pour her full of the same.

I pull my map from the pack and unfold it to see just where I will leave the Trail if I decide to join the Gathering for a day or two. My finger is tracing the route when a truck zooms by and honks. Sarah and Tripper John, sitting in the back like the happiest cargo on earth, wave and vanish down the road. I feel left behind with too far to go.

That evening it begins a slow steady drizzle and I buy a half pint of bourbon. From time to time, I take a sip in the cold wind. It burns as it runs down my throat, but it warms my insides. I begin to feel holy.

The sun is going down when a car stops with two women in their early twenties. Both are almost as pretty as Sarah and the one with crow-black hair has a pierced nose with a tiny gold ring.

Need a ride to the Gathering? she says.

When I was caught in the thunderstorm and lightning flashed all around, I was tempted to take a ride when someone stopped. I'm almost as tempted now. It's hard to say no to pleasure when it sends a limo to pick you up. I explain why I'm walking.

Whatever makes your blood run, she says. If you change your mind, we'll see you there.

As their red taillights disappear into the twilight I wonder if I'm a bit crazy for not going with them. I could've gone and stayed a day or two and gotten a ride back to the Trail where they picked me up. Like it or not, I'm totally obsessed with the walk by now. Then, too, as far as the women, I may not be as free as I once thought I was. I keep seeing the face of Venda and hearing her moans when we kissed on the blanket by the great bubbling spring, shooting from deep within the earth. Still, Venda is not here and I may never see her again.

It's a fine line between twilight and darkness when I approach a swamp thick with towering cypress. It continues to drizzle and it's getting colder. I raise the half pint of Bourbon to my lips and drain the last few drops. Slipping the bottle into my leather jacket, I enter the swamp and get goose bumps when two cranes fly over. They are so faint against the darkening sky that they seem like little more than spirits arising from the rain itself. They both excite me and fill me with the mystery and sadness I experienced when I was a child and my father and two other men shot a crane in the woods. It tumbled to the earth and we ran to it. When I saw it was dead, the magic vanished and I did not understand why they cut its wing off and stuffed it into a hunting jacket. To this day I believe some part of me is still trying to breathe life back into that bird.

As the two cranes blend into the night I begin to chant. It is a song that comes from feelings stored in my body and soul from all those I've met so far on the walk. It is the only way I know at times to deal with so many emotions at once. Each time I chant, the song is slightly different than before because each day new people—new tones—are added to make my voice rise and fall at new places. Then, too, there are moments like now, when I sense or imagine—it really doesn't matter which—that I am in touch with the spirits of the Cherokee who walked this very Trail. If I am only and simply in touch with a single spirit, the human spirit within, that's okay too. Anything that allows me naturally to transcend the earthly plane so that I may return better to grasp and savor my flesh-and-bones reality, I welcome with both arms wide open.

As I chant in the darkness of the swamp I become too taken by the feelings to contain it in a song. My knees begin to reach for the treetops and my elbows go up and down as if I have wings to carry me into the sky where the cranes marked a trail in the rain. I am a man in a glorious frenzy, dancing and chanting among the trees, swaying in the wind. There is no doubt about my freedom and I do not long for woman, home, or a soft warm bed. I am as complete as a man can be. I am a song pulsating in the night from the roots of a tree up through the rain and into the stars. If only the cranes can hear me, I don't care. I'm alive. For a while, I'm alive.

# CHAPTER TWENTY-EIGHT

THERE IS LITTLE that's spiritual or mystical the next day, when I drag into Golconda on the Ohio River. There doesn't have to be either for me to feel full. I'm just so happy to arrive, after walking twenty-five miles, and get a room. Ironically, I get it in the Rainbow Inn, high upon a hill overlooking the river. The inn was built in 1867 as a boardinghouse for high school girls. It's been left plain and simple. I like that it smells old too. The owner, Dan Woods, is an Indian, a Choctaw, who grew up in Oklahoma. He broadcasts a radio show from his bedroom five mornings a week and his listeners know him as Deuteronomy Dan. He lives in the house across the road.

Don't let the name fool you, says Dan. I don't try to push my beliefs on another man.

Deuteronomy Dan, retired from the navy, is one of eleven
children. He almost died of diphtheria when he was a baby.

My parents had just about given up all hope, he says. Then
this old horse doctor came to look at me. Said he only knew one
possible cure, and that it might kill me. Well, what could my
folks do? They gave the go ahead and the old man gave me horse
blood. I was taken home and before the night was out I started to
swell up like a balloon. I was rushed back to the old horse doctor. Know what he claimed?

No, I say, a bit dumbfounded and amused.

He said, Deuteronomy Dan continues, that he forgot to tell
'em that swelling was a sure sign that I was gonna make it. He
also predicted how I'd be for years to come. I was a runt, no
bigger than a mean dog, till I was thirteen. Then I started growing
so fast I'd wake up in the middle of the night with my whole
body hurting. Now, can you beat that, just some old horse blood?


Steps stretch from the yard of the inn, surrounded by massive oaks, down the hill to a street some fifty or sixty yards away. I
take those steps as night falls, to find a café. The wind blows and
red and yellow leaves drift into the twilight. Golconda is the
perfect place to rest for a couple of days. There's not a single
traffic light in town, or the whole county for that matter, and an
old courthouse in the center of town is the only public building
that offers a third floor. The two big thrills of the year are the deer
hunting and bass fishing tournaments, the latter going on right
now.

Lights begin to come on inside houses and it's hard to imagine crime in any form or fashion in Golconda. Built in the very
southern tip of Illinois, between the Mississippi and Ohio rivers,
without a bridge to connect it to Kentucky just a half mile away,

it's like a hideout from the rest of the world. There are times when a man feels that he is exactly where he should be, and this is true for me right now.

Even the simple food, a bowl of white beans and corn bread with sliced onion, at the Dari Bar strikes the perfect note in my journey tonight. Those eating at the tables around me are all country people, and the simplicity helps ground me and make me feel safe and in touch with my roots, just as Tripper John and sensual Sarah fed my wilder, bohemian side. The waitress eyes my empty bowl.

Want me to fill it up? she says.

Is the second bowl the same price? I ask.

No. She smiles. It's free.

I hand her the bowl and she disappears into the kitchen. It takes so little sometimes to become part of the human race; I get a bit choked up that Americans can be so warm and giving. I think this is what's moving me more than anything else on the walk. *I am connected to everybody.* It's as simple as ABC, but in my wandering lifestyle and eccentric and isolated ways I had forgotten that, not in my mind but where it really counts—in my heart. Call me a real sap tonight, but when the waitress returns with my bowl filled with beans, I want to reach up and stroke her arm. I chicken out and hide behind words.

You're a good waitress, I tell her.

You think so? she says.

She's a pretty woman, around forty, but it's clear that she's not very happy. She looks tired and maybe a bit lonely.

I've been watching you, I say. You're good with people. You care.

I try, she says. But Mama don't think I'm very good. No matter how hard I try, I just ain't fast enough.

Guess that depends on where you want to go, I say.

Yeah. She smiles. Guess it does at that. Mostly I just want to
go home and rest my feet. Did you want another slice of onion?

Yes, I say. Thanks.

The waitress goes to get the onion. A man with a hat with a
fishing fly on it turns around at the table next to mine. He rubs
his beard and lowers a cup of coffee from his lips.

Well, he says. What d'you think? Will the fish be hitting
tomorrow or not?

Hope so, I say.

Me too, he says, sipping the coffee. But I ain't holding my
breath. I fished all day and didn't catch but two about the size of
my hand. Course, half the time I was busy getting my grandson's
line untangled. Whole other story last month. I went out at dawn
and the fish did everything but hop in the boat and bait my hook.
I had two lines out and couldn't take one off the hook before the
other line went to jerking. I think this rain has them spooked.
Fish are like women. They ain't themselves if the weather ain't
just so.

The waitress brings another slice of onion. As I finish the
beans I can't help but wonder how the Gathering is going for
Tripper John and Sarah. The aggressive young woman with the
tiny gold ring in her nose also crosses my mind. I have no doubt
that her cup is full and her blanket is warm by now. I'm still
pleased, at least for the hour, that I came on to Golconda instead
of turning north for the Gathering. But it also excites me that, if I
so decide, I can thumb there tomorrow and spend just the day, to
return to the inn at night. To have constant options has to be one
of man's greatest gifts. I can't imagine living a routine that
wouldn't allow such choices. God, I feel wealthy tonight. Yeah, I
think I'll order a piece of chocolate pie.

* * *

I leave the café and wander through downtown. It's so small I have to stop and turn around to make sure I just passed it. I peek through the window at a bar where several fishermen gather to lie about the big ones that got away. I'm too full from the beans and pie to have a drink, and besides, I want to be alone to savor the peace that comes from walking all day.

I walk down to the Ohio River and it grabs me for the first time that I won't have a bridge to help me over into Kentucky. I'll have to get a ride with a fisherman.

The wind coming off the river is cold and wet, but I like that it makes me appreciate my own body heat trapped inside my leather jacket, which I bought in a thrift store for two bucks last year. I even like that my face is becoming a little numb, because I know how good it will feel to get warm once I'm back at the inn.

Kentucky. It's hard to believe that it's just across the river. Once I set foot on its soil I'm back in the South. Not the Deep South where I call home, but close enough to give me chills as I begin to imagine my cabin waiting for me on that hill between Lookout and Sand mountains. Dear sweet feet and body, don't fail me now.


I head for the inn with hopes of finding an old movie on the TV that sits in the small lobby just outside my door. I admit it, I want to escape for a while and not think about all the people I've met. I'm so packed with their pains and joys and my hating to part with people on the Trail that my nerves are stretched as tight as the strings on a violin. Or a banged-up guitar. This isn't a contradiction to the peace I spoke of earlier. I simply know when I've reached my saturation point with people.

As I climb the great flight of steps from the town up to the inn I cross my fingers that I'll find a movie with Humphrey Bo-

gart or Jimmy Stewart. Most of today's TV heroes don't do a lot
for me. No great charisma. No deep character.

The largest oak I've ever seen in my life sits in the yard of
Deuteronomy Dan. It's almost big enough for a tunnel to let a
VW pass. Its limbs reach across the road to the inn, which I now
enter, an old romantic movie still on my mind.

But I'm disappointed. The lobby is occupied by five members of the Green family, in town for a reunion. The mother is
eighty-nine and held captive by her youngest son, forty-seven,
who wears a Louisiana prison-guard uniform and tells a story
with the passion of a madman as his older brother and two sisters
listen.

If you're wondering about the guard uniform, he says, I wear
it because I don't have any other clothes. I work as a braille
transcriber. Have a seat. I was telling them about my wife. She
died two weeks ago.

Mr. Green is, frankly, an ugly man with glasses. He's also
just enough overweight to make anyone who's picky about fat
turn his head. I find his face a treasure of expressions.

I'm sorry to hear that, I say, sensing I should go to my room
right this second before I get hooked on his heartbreak story.

She was a good woman, he continues. If it hadn't been for
her, I'd still be in prison. I did fifteen years in California for
writing hot checks.

It's true, laughs his mother. It sent me to a shrink.

Yeah, says her son, I was a real bastard.

How about that time, says his sister without a hint of resent-
ment, that I gave blood, trying to get enough money to cover a
bad check?

Okay, he adds. It's established that I was a rat, so let's move
on. As I was saying, my wife died two weeks ago. She was blind,
but never complained a day of her life. The most thankful person

that ever walked the face of the earth. She had been operated on four times for cancer over a period of several years. Then a few months ago they found a knot on the back of her leg. Before that was cut out, though, they found a new growth at the base of her head. The doc went in with a laser, but the growth was so wrapped around her spinal cord, there wasn't a prayer. A week later a roar began in her ears and she couldn't hear. She couldn't see or hear and the only way we could communicate was through braille.

He pauses as if to find the courage to go on. His family, and especially his mother, wait with what surely must be some of the greatest patience I've ever seen in human beings. He takes his glasses from his face, wipes them with a dirty handkerchief, and returns them to his nose as if he can now see with some new meaning.

Well, he says, she was a dead woman still breathing. Locked inside a room no bigger than her skull with a train roaring through it twenty-four hours a day. Only one thing kept her going. She was waiting on her first grandchild to be born. It was a girl and I never saw her so happy. She sat in a rocking chair and held her naked for three hours. *Three whole hours* she explored that baby with her fingertips. She counted her toes and fingers over and over. She felt her mouth, her nose, eyes and ears like she'd never seen anything like them before. She hummed a song too. A song that just came from her insides for that baby. The next day she died.

I'm not sure why I'm usually compelled to respond to people's down-and-out stories. I certainly don't think it's a strength. Maybe I just say something so the silence won't gain more power.

She was an exceptional woman, I say, rising from my chair and stepping toward my door only four or five feet away.

Don't you want to hear how we met? he says.

I'd be a better listener tomorrow, I say. I'm pretty beat tonight.

Before he has a chance to hook me again I tell them good night and disappear into my room. Long after I'm in bed I still see his wife holding the naked baby in her lap as her fingertips count tiny toes and gently rest on the heartbeat in the soft spot in the center of the head. Between each heartbeat, as the delicate skin rises and falls, an owl hoots in the massive and ancient oak outside my window. I'm so tired that I fall asleep floating through the woods with a baby in my arms. Sometime in the night I half awaken and count my fingers before I realize I can see. Some movie this turns out to be.

# CHAPTER TWENTY-NINE

THE RAIN PASSES in the night and the next morning, Saturday, Golconda jumps with fishermen in town to snag the prize money. The cool air is so fresh and I'm so rested that I feel like I could almost swim the Ohio with the pack on my back. The real joy of the day is that I don't have to walk from sunrise to sunset. I can be a bum all day and do whatever I want. Mainly, I'm just pleased to look at the sky. It's so big and blue and powerful despite its illusion of peace. For several days now I have been experiencing something totally new with the sky. When I'm inside, even with the curtains drawn, I still see it. I don't have a ceiling over me. I have breathtaking blue sky. I'm bonding with it in a way I did not know was possible. It fills me with hope and a sense of eternity. Ah, yes, to awake refreshed on top of the world and clothed in sky on the Ohio River is one of the greatest mornings of my life. Then a

subtle fear sets in: As much as I long for home, at times I don't
want the journey to end. I don't want to become just another man
wearing clothes that can be washed at an all-night Laundromat.
How will I preserve these rare feelings that take me to a higher
plane? My God, what does it really say about me—or the modern
world—even to concern myself with such things already? But it's
true. I can already hear the teeth of the Great Machine grinding
away as it opens its monstrous mouth in the shopping centers
and on oil slicks washing onto beaches where seals and otters
and ducks squirm in black tar. Stuck between those giant teeth I
see people dangling with Visas and MasterCards, while new cars
roll forward from the throat and down the tongue onto our highways lined with gas stations, like a rash along the spinal cord of a
back so bent it may at any moment break. But don't worry, this is
just some old stuff in my head. Everything is really just fine and
dandy. Nothing to get alarmed about.


Following breakfast, I go into a junk and antique store where
an old woman unloads boxes of vases. She has the most interesting sneeze I've heard all day.

Oh, she sighs, I want to believe it's the dust. But I'm afraid
it's not. Only October and already I have a cold. Catch anything
this morning?

Nothing but some sleep, I say. I'm not here to fish. You have
any Indian relics?

Over here in this box, she says, are a few pieces. I just
bought them a couple of days ago.

She leads me to a box and pulls out a few arrowheads and a
small, grooved stone axe. It's chipped on one end, but I always
get excited when I hold such a piece. Who made it over 1,000
years ago, what was he like, and how did he die?

You know Ray Morris? I say, examining the relic as if it can pass on some wisdom simply by touching it.

Oh, yes, she says. Everybody in town knows him. He put together that wagon train last year and went all the way from somewhere in Tennessee to Oklahoma, along the Trail of Tears. Know what that is?

I've heard of it, I say.

Well, she says, it—well, I'll be. There's Ray now, across the street.

I place the stone axe back in the box and hurry outside. I'd been hearing of Ray Morris ever since I started walking and had phoned him this morning, but no one was home. Yes, maybe it's nothing more than another ten-cent coincidence that I was holding the Indian relic when I asked about him and he appeared. Maybe not. Dr. Noble had said that there's no such thing as coincidence. Be that the case or not, it's a perfect time to confess the outcome of two experiments I ran back in Tahlequah, where the little redheaded girl tried sorcery on me.

The day I met Dr. Noble, he took me to the house of Jane Osti, a Cherokee in the Paint Clan. She was about my age and as soon as we saw each other we felt a rare connection and said so. Her ancestors lived only forty miles from my cabin when they were given the red carpet to Oklahoma in 1838. We had a drink and she showed me her artwork, offering a piece of bronze from a new sculpture, the giant head of an Indian woman, for the burial ritual. Anyway, she had an appointment and we had to part. Both of us assumed we'd see each other again. The next day I phoned her, but she wasn't home. I started walking toward the Indian dances three miles from town. I felt I had entered a fertile realm for communication in Tahlequah and begin to envision Jane. I also started to chant, quietly and to myself, for five minutes. I finally stopped and was amused at myself. Then a car pulled over. Jane was driving. We spent the afternoon together and went to her house for lunch. Everything was fine till her boyfriend, Richard, showed up. (His sister, Willma Mankiller, is the first female chief of the Cherokee Nation.) His people came from Alabama where I live, and I tried to connect, but oh well, we all know what it's like to show up unannounced at a lover's house and find strange company.

I went back to the center of Tahlequah and sat on a bench in front of the old courthouse surrounded by trees. I was feeling a bit lonely and eating an apple, when I began to think of Steve Garrett, a Cherokee student I had met the day before, who went to Jane Osti's house with Dr. Noble and myself. He had a great sense of humor and played in a rock and roll band. So there I was on the bench with nothing more exciting than an apple to talk to when I decided to try the experiment again. I didn't chant this time, but I envisioned Steve walking down the sidewalk till I could almost see him. When I did really see him only four or five minutes later walking down the very sidewalk I had imagined him on, I almost fell off the bench. Coincidence? Who the hell knows for sure?

You're Ray Morris? I say, eyeing the man who organized and led an entire wagon train along the Trail of Tears last year.

Ray, in his early fifties, stands over six feet tall and wears a cowboy hat with a single delicate feather from a redbird stuck in the band. He eyes my crow, wild turkey, and blue jay feathers sticking from my hat with the snake rattler.

*Yeah?* he says, fishing an old silver lighter from his pocket. He flips it open with such grace and speed that I can't help but picture a gambler in a forties Western. Then, as he strikes the lighter, he raises his coat to guard the flame from the wind. Lighting the cigarette, he blows a puff of smoke and lowers the coat. I don't smoke and generally can't stand to breathe when someone else is doing so within a few feet, but as this first whiff of tobacco hits my nose I'm transposed back to childhood, when I believed smoking was all-magical and powerful, like I thought adults to be. So here, for a split second, I stand in awe of the Marlboro Man, who somehow has stepped out of the billboard and onto the Trail of Tears.

My name is Jerry Ellis, I say. I've been wanting to meet you ever since I read about you in a newspaper article I found on the wall inside the Old Baptist Mission Church, on my second day on the Trail. I'm walking the old route to my home in Alabama.

Ray's eyes now squint and I'm not sure if it's him or me, but I smell competition in the air. He takes another drag off the cigarette and blows smoke into the wind. It's another of endless lessons in the Law of Expectations. Don't ever have any when it comes to how people will respond. I had imagined that we would feel an instant connection and celebrate it with overflowing excitement and joy.

I don't have time right now, says Ray. If you want to talk, your best bet is to load your ass into my truck here and go with me. I have some business to tend to.

I have plans right now, I say. Maybe later?

We confirm each other's phone numbers and he drives away. I lay ten to one that he won't phone. What bothers me more than that is that I probably won't phone him either. Ah, yes, how quickly a billboard dream fades. If only I could master the fine art of being a man and a child in the same breath—and sometimes I'm lucky enough to do so—I could stay amused at men's egos, including my own, every waking hour.

I can't shake the brief meeting with Ray. I feel like I failed somehow. How could two men take the same Trail and not share a little of the same blood? Worse yet, I begin to consider that he was responding to some subtle but strong attitude I may have projected without realizing it.

The next day, Sunday, church bells ring to liven Golconda as an October Festival gets under way around the old courthouse. It's here that I spot Ray again. He stands by his covered wagon, which traveled over eight hundred miles. He sees me, I'm sure, but doesn't let on. I'm not sure how, but I'm determined to find our bridge.

I phoned your house last night, I say. But no one answered.

I got in late, he says, flipping open his already-famous lighter and raising his coat to flame a cigarette.

This is some wagon, I say. What was the biggest problem you had with it on the Trail?

What *kind* of problem? he says, his tone on edge.

- I see how he may think I'm wanting to step into the darkness with a question that implies there was any trouble at all. But this isn't my intent in the least.

I've never had experience with a wagon, I say. Never even rode on one. Just thought I might learn something from you.

His eyes now soften and I feel a bridge rising from the water to connect us. He pulls on his cigarette with a new ease.

The brakes, he says. They kept wearing thin. There were fifteen or sixteen wagons on the trip, but this was the only one actually from the 1800s.

I walk over to the brakes as if standing next to them will show me a picture of what happened on the trip. But I'm really just making sure that Ray sees that I'm truly interested. Now, as if it's taken twenty-four hours to complete some mental orbit, he responds to what I'm doing.

Had a guy back in Tennessee, says Ray, who wanted to walk
the Trail as we came across on the wagons. We were knocking
out thirty to thirty-five miles a day, so he had to maintain a slow
run to stay up. He was an insurance salesman and by the end
of the first day, his feet were covered with blisters. He ended up
just stuffing his shoes full of Vaseline, like he was greasing a
wagon wheel. How are you crossing the river?

Hoping to find a fisherman to take me across, I say.

You know the Indians crossed by flatboat? he says. White
men could bring a whole wagon over for 12½ cents, but the
Cherokee got nailed a dollar per head.

Ray, a county agent for the Agriculture Department, worked
for seven years on an Indian reservation in Washington. He
adopted his teenage son there and he and his wife are foster
parents for two girls, who are playing around the wagon.

They've been molested, he says. But they're doing pretty
good right now. I don't know what the country's coming to with
our children though. The media's got this whole molestation
thing so sensationalized that children are afraid of strangers. Hell,
people are gregarious by nature. We're becoming so afraid of each
other we can't even say what we really think and feel anymore.
What will kids grow up to believe about the world?

In a world of slick salesmen who calculate every word and
gesture to manipulate the would-be buyer—even if the product is
the desperate need to be accepted—it's refreshing to hear Ray
speak his mind and not give a shit whether I agree with him or
not. He's as rugged and straightforward as the wagon-master job
he took on to lead the train across eight states.

Children are and always have been, says Ray, our only hope
for a better world. When we crossed the country on wagons we
visited every school we could, to educate the kids. We talked to
over fifty thousand of 'em. The media doing you okay? *USA Today*

put our picture on the front page and did a damn good story. But some of the papers questioned what we were doing. Talked about trash they claimed we left where we camped, instead of getting information to the public. By the time we got to Oklahoma, some of the people had dropped out and a lot of the others were questioning themselves. It was cold and snow was coming down. We even got mixed reactions in Tahlequah. Some of the Cherokee thought we should let the past stay buried. I think it brought back too much pain and sadness for some of them.

Ray, the indestructible Marlboro Man, now becomes vulnerable and I see the child in him. This, of course, only makes him more likable. Thank goodness, we found our bridge. Even if this link of people I'm joining along the Trail is as thin and fragile as a single thread of spiderweb, Ray is a great and important addition to the circle. In my mind, we are sitting around the eternal flame, our prayers rising on smoke to the Great Spirit.

# CHAPTER THIRTY

T HE FOLLOWING MORNING I walk into town to have breakfast, and phone Ray from Golconda's only outdoor phone booth. He had invited me to spend the night with him and his family last night, but I had already paid Deuteronomy Dan for another day. I'm disappointed that Ray doesn't answer, and hang up the phone to return to my room and pack to head for Kentucky. I find Deuteronomy Dan walking around the massive oak outside his house as if looking for a decision.

Lose something? I say.

I'm thinking about having it cut, he says. It's not that I want to. But the storms—all of 'em come right through here and . . .

He motions that the tree may one day crash into the inn. The oak must be at least two hundred years old, which means it was already a big tree when the Indians passed through here and camped, according to three elderly sisters who were in the inn last night from Arkansas to visit the ashes of the Golconda home where they were born and raised, just on the next hill.

My grandmother, said the oldest sister, saw the Cherokee when she was only a girl. She had gone with her mother in the snow to give food to them, and a little Indian girl gave her a doll. I wish it had been passed on and we had it today. The things that get lost, I'll swear.

This is the first time I've spent three days anywhere on the walk, and though my back and leg continue to trouble me, I'm rested and eager to cross the Ohio River. As I enter town I reach into my pocket for a quarter to call Ray. But guess what? I find him standing in the phone booth where I called him less than an hour ago. He offers to hang up as I approach him, but I simply shake his hand and keep going. I am, it seems, in rhythm and don't want to break it.


As I near the docks I become concerned that I may be stuck waiting for a ride to Kentucky because I see only a single boat in use. It's Monday and even fishermen have to work from time to time. But luck is on my side and Lloyd Brown, casting from a lone boat, offers to zip me across the river.

This too fast for you? he says.

No, I say. I like it fast.

But I'm also a bit afraid. His small flatboat bounces across the roaring river, where waves crash into clouds of mist, soaking my face. I try to look as calm as the giant oak Deuteronomy Dan plans to cut to the ground, but my hand stays tight around the life preserver under my leg. I imagine us flipping over into the icy water.

How deep is it here? I say.

I'm surprised when Lloyd—he calls himself River Rat—jerks a piece of cloth from a depth finder. He flips a switch and squints for exactness.

Almost fifty feet, he shouts over the boat's motor. See that dot there? That's a catfish. Big as my leg too.

As we near the Kentucky side of the river I turn back to watch Golconda become a thing of the past. For a fleeting moment I imagine an Indian on the hill. Then he is nothing more than a limb on a tree. Is the entire tree actually a tribe in disguise?

Lloyd eases the front of his boat onto the bank and I pull out my wallet to pay the five bucks I promised for the ride. He won't even look at it and motions for me to get it out of sight as if such things get tangled up in his line. The boat rocks and I feel like I'm walking on ice as I step toward the shore, the heavy pack in my hand throwing me off balance. But my foot finds the sweet earth before I fall. Lloyd pushes from the bank to skid back across the river and become little more than a cigar box by the time I walk a hundred yards into Kentucky, away from the heartland of America and into the progressive and crumbling South.

The Trail is only a dirt road here and the trees are the tallest I've seen since I left the mountains of Alabama. They cover me with red and golden leaves, flickering blue as the wind parts the limbs for the sky to loom down and lift my feet toward home. Poison ivy vines up a dogwood to create a red trail so inviting that I almost forget its danger and want to touch it to see if it feels as beautiful as it looks. When the Cherokee came upon such a plant they talked to it, addressing it as friend, with the hope, of course, that it wouldn't hurt them. But even a friend can sometimes get under the skin, and that's when they reached for the crawfish meat.

This area is so remote that I easily imagine I'm walking 150 years ago. It fills me with that great sense of power that comes from forgetting the contemporary world. I do not, however, pretend that I want to live like this all the time and turn my back on the fascinating age in which I live. To do so would be, in my opinion, as dangerous as those who deny their ancestral past and all its spiritual connections to the earth, rivers, fire,—well, you see the direction in which I'm looking. To dismiss this as simply some romantic notion is to deny death itself, for in the end aren't we—as the song says—only dust in the wind ? If it seems that I'm asking the impossible—for man to undergo some great spiritual revolution and reconnect with his soul and environment and, indeed, his fellow man—it's just that I am now entering a new phase of the walk, where I imagine that I am being granted insights into the state of mankind in America. All this walking in Nature and connecting with strangers is tearing my walls down. I have only the thinnest of membranes around me now and I am a receptor, if not for that racing creature called *truth,* then at least for that fleeting creature called *hope.* In other words, it's a helluva good day on the Trail of Tears.

Within an hour's walk from the Ohio River, I turn to my right down another dirt road into a forest toward Mantle Rock, where the Indians camped for days, waiting for the river to become free of floating ice so they could cross. I'm only some twenty-five yards into the woods when I hear something or someone running my way.

I freeze, and the snap of twigs and the rustle of leaves become louder. I gaze into the forest and my eyes try to focus as a hint of fear joins company with the excitement that the unexpected is headed straight for me. Then, as if rising right up from the earth itself, I stand face-to-face with a great buck, its antlers as grand and sharp as its eyes are delicate and holy. As if trying to see into each other, we stare, caught it seems in an eternal breath connecting two worlds. Man to Nature. But, finally, his nostrils spread, and *zap,* he's only a white tail and then nothing more than bushes quivering from his flight, to leave me like little more than a big rock.

Adrenaline still shooting through my heart with the speed of a hawk dipping from the sky to snatch a mouse from a field, I lift my foot to go deeper into the forest, only to see yet another great sight. A wild-turkey gobbler, some thirty or forty yards away, struts his magnificent tail feathers while three hens peck acorns from the ground. The wind is just right for me to watch them as if I'm nothing more than a fork in a tree. I figure the deer had been spooked by the gobbler and that's why he almost ran into me. It strikes me with the wonder of a child's secret that I have a turkey feather in my hat as I study the gobbler still strutting about his hens. I'd give my front crooked tooth if I could gobble right now to see the birds' response. But they see me soon enough and disappear so quickly that they seem to transform into fallen leaves, hiding on the ground somewhere among their tracks.

I walk to where I saw the birds in hopes of finding some beautiful feathers, but none are here. I march deeper into the woods.

When I first spot Mantle Rock, it awes me even more than the deer and the turkeys. It's a great bridge of stone, rising from the earth some ten to twelve feet and stretching the length of a dozen horses. Its backside is also stone and its east end tapers into the moist earth. Compared to camping in the woods, I see how it made excellent shelter for the Cherokee and much earlier Indians who had never heard of white men, let alone anything as wild and nightmarish as being moved to another home.

I set down my pack and move about the shelter to squat here and there against a rock wall. When the Cherokee huddled here from the snow and blowing wind, they would've been so packed that body heat would've been a blessing. But I'm not comforted by this thought for long when I see how, in a way, it was like a train car packed with Jews on the way to a death camp.

I'm tempted to camp here for the night, but it's not even noon yet and I'm still on fire with energy. From my pack, I remove seven acorns I gathered under Deuteronomy Dan's oak. (Seven was a magic number to the Cherokee and they often used it in rituals, as well as building their longhouses with that many sides.) I bury the acorns deep in the soil for next spring and take off. If Deuteronomy Dan's oak must bite the dust, then maybe an offspring will furnish a place for birds and squirrels to hide from man.

Joy, Kentucky, is so small, that next to it Golconda could pass as Swinging Sin City. It's here that I meet Beverly Crittenden, eighty-two years old, sitting outside her garage with her dear friends, Sweet Talker and Pretty Thing, two ten-year-old roosters.

The pack too heavy to carry all the way up here? she snaps.

I let the pack ease onto the ground near the Trail. I like that she has challenge in her bones.

Well, I say. I didn't want to bring it to the house first thing. I was afraid you might see my plan to move in with you.

She's an old woman, but her eyes are as sharp and alert as those of a twenty-five year old. It's also clear that she's watching my eyes to see what I'm made of. A self-proclaimed old maid, she taught school fifteen years and then decided money was more fun than kids; she became a banker till she retired. That garden spot down there? Yeah, she plows it, plants it, and picks it.

I canned 342 jars this summer, she says. Why shouldn't I? If you slow down *too* much, you dry up and blow away. But you were asking me about Mantle Rock. I played there when I was a little girl. Found lots of artifacts too. A couple of years ago, the last time I was down there—back before my leg went out on me —my heart just broke. Somebody had gone in there at night with a bulldozer and unearthed the Cherokee graves. And for what? They didn't have anything when they passed through here.

Why do you call the rooster Sweet Talker? I say.

Because that's what he does, Beverly snaps. He gives me pretty songs.

You mean he crows? I say.

Now, you know that's not what I mean, she says. You heard him crow already. He *sings* too. You want to see?

Her right leg is lame and her brace broke a few days ago. She comes from her chair and must walk on her right ankle to reach for Sweet Talker. He walks backwards because, according to Beverly, he was pecked too much when he was a chick. She finally talks him into her hands and lifts him as if he's part of the Greatest Show on Earth.

Show him, she whispers. Show him how you can sing. Go on, don't be afraid. Yes, my precious Sweet Talker. Such a pretty bird. Won't you sing for me? Come on—she whispers ever more softly—you show him how you can sing such pretty songs.

As if understanding the old woman, the rooster finally begins to make a delicate clucking sound. It's no nightingale, but the way she holds him and looks at him creates the rarest of songs. Within her private dreams he seems to fly her way beyond her wrinkles and crippled leg and I guess it's true that we get love wherever we can find it.

You want to see my canned goods? says Beverly, lowering Sweet Talker to the ground.

We go inside and she opens the door to the cellar. She refuses to let me help her as she must go backwards down the stairs just like Sweet Talker did on the ground when she first tried to catch him.

If Sweet Talker is her best friend, then these towering shelves of canned fruits, vegetables, jellies, and jams are her children. Standing next to them, but sure not to block any of them, she is a prideful queen. (Later, down the road, I will learn from a woman that two years ago Beverly was mowing her lawn and stopped to move a limb when the mower sucked her long hair into it and wrapped it around the blade. She was caught in that position for two hours before someone came to the rescue.)

You're a regular canning factory, I say.

We go back upstairs and she shows me the relics she found at Mantle Rock when she was a child. They're some of the best spearheads I've ever seen. I'm so involved with examining them that she finally takes them from me and closes the drawer where she keeps them. I take the gesture as a hint to leave, but when I say as much she begins to drag out old bottles and fans—anything that's old and unusual, to hold my attention. For the first time, when I again tell her I must go, she drops her mask.

I don't get to talk to many people, she says.

# CHAPTER THIRTY-ONE

THE KENTUCKY COUNTRYSIDE is alive with rolling hills and barn lofts, hanging thick with tobacco plants turned upside down to cure as small, steady fires burn on the ground to keep moisture away. Smoke rises from the barns' tin roofs to fill the evening air with aromatic tease. I don't at all associate it with cigarettes or cigars. Rather, it's as if tobacco is something from the gods and people store it in its own special house while it transforms into something sacred and medicinal.

The night's beauty becomes stronger when the orange harvest moon rises atop a hay field and the smell of the smoke blends with the cool moist air. Except for an occasional light in a distant farmhouse, there's no sign of human life. It seems as though the moon shines for me and me alone. This is no longer a walk. I have gone beyond the point of no return into an odyssey.

Maybe it happened before tonight and I simply wasn't aware of it. Like falling in love, maybe such a thing happens little by little, till a man is over the edge. In any event, I have, for at least this phase of my life, found my form. The middle-aged crisis, if that's what it ever was, is passing. I don't understand it, but I am no longer afraid of dying. Perhaps it's simply because I am doing exactly what I want to and feel good about it that makes me whole. Still, as happened just a few days ago when everything was so solid, I'm hit with a gnawing anxiety. What happens when the odyssey ends? What do I do next to keep life this fulfilling and exciting?

The great harvest moon takes my mind off itself and I get lost again in the night's sweet tobacco. A new barn—not used for curing—appears and I wish Venda were here. We'd climb to the loft and build a cocoon in the hay. I have no doubt that her lips, nipples, and more could transform me in the dark into a fox or a wolf or a snake. If I simply remained a man who could explore her from head to foot with my tongue, that would be okay too.

But *something* is off, or different, tonight that I can't yet put my finger on. I've been walking for over an hour in the moonlight and find what I think is a good place to camp in a field near a grove of oaks. An owl hoots nearby and it seems safe here. But once I begin unpacking the tent, I get the feeling I should move on. I obey and head down the Trail for another mile or so. I begin to pitch the tent again and the feeling returns. Not a single time before tonight have I unpacked my tent and not camped where my feet marked the spot.

But I once more repack the tent and walk on through the moonlight. This is no big deal, but I'm not sure what's going on with my instincts—if that's what it is—to keep me moving. Am I going *away* from something or *toward* something in the night? In any event, I find a third spot and this one is just right. I crawl into the tent, take off my clothes, and slide into the sleeping bag. I'm atop grass eight to ten inches thick and the bed is wonderfully soft. The moon shines through the nylon and my little net window to make a perfect home.

My body and mind begin to dissolve into one with the moon, smoke from the barns, the day's journey across the great Ohio River, the buck, turkeys, Mantle Rock, and of course, Beverly with her Sweet Talker and cellar kingdom of fruits and vegetables. Then I see myself walking the Trail to Mantle Rock; I feel where I squatted in the shadows, the sky another world up there beyond the trees. Then I experience something I have never known before:

I begin either to fall asleep or step further into the odyssey that now owns me. My chest feels as if it is no longer skin and bones, but a delicate membrane which opens, not unlike a tender mouth about to kiss, and into it comes a floating tribe of marching Indians made of pale blue lights. Startled, to say the least, I rise from the grass bed with the belief that such a thing —surely mere images so close to the conscious mind that they couldn't wait for deep sleep to play—will fade instantly and I will again have at least the illusion that I am in control of my life. But the faint blue luminous figures, mostly children, do not cooperate with my reflex logic. As gently as the smoke rises from the barns' exotic leaves, they continue to walk floating into my chest, into my heart. I have only the moon to console me, and its harvest light seems concerned with the sole purpose of empowering the ghosts or spirits or whatever they are to march forward into my both frightened and transfixed being. It all lasts only a few seconds—oh, doesn't time make some changes on an odyssey—but before *they* vanish I have the merciful opportunity to be both involved and outside the rare event in the same breath. Not unlike an orgasm, but in this case a spiritual one, I feel its beginning and know I can only go with it, though it seems of another world or another dimension.

I am left sitting up as if awaiting an explanation. I tell myself that *they* were simply a flash dream that lingered. I had fallen asleep without realizing it. Everything on the journey has become so magnified that this is only another example of man's ability—and need—to enrich his trace of existence. *I'm not just a man. I'm a part of God, with magical and mystical powers. I won't die and simply become dust. I will live forever.* But even a loner, priding himself on individuality, will sometimes try to direct himself back toward the herd if he feels he is wandering too far away from accepted reality.

But, no, even if I am far, far away from the crowd, I won't lie to myself here and now. I made contact with *them,* or *something,* in a realm as real as the earth to which we all return. They are in me now. They are part of my soul. Does this mean that the vision I had years ago is coming true, or am I simply a desperate and poetic misfit in a sometimes less-than-hilarious high-tech world?

I had a vision four years ago when, near my cabin, a reservoir was being built for Fort Payne. A giant yellow dozer had scraped the earth to go back in time hundreds, if not thousands, of years. The workmen had left for the day and I arrived to hunt for relics. I soon discovered that a grave had been uncovered. I found a leg bone, stone tomahawk, celt, and arrowhead within a six-foot circle.

I buried the bone, but went home with the artifacts. This happened on a day when I was giving my heart and soul to writing a screenplay about a Cherokee who returned to the mountains after getting lost as a cabaret dancer in the wild and worldly lifestyle of New Orleans. He returned to his homeland to

seek his soul and entered a cave where his ancestors hid to escape capture on the Trail of Tears. While in this cave, he built a
fire and sang in hopes of calling forth the spirit of his grandfather,
a shaman, who had told him as a child that the day would come
when he must undergo a great trial to prove his worth to *see* the
Spirit World, or be lost forever in the white man's world of mass-
produced garbage and all it represented. Finally, the grandfather
*did* appear from the shadows of the cave. He was a faint blue light
and pointed to the west, only to point again to the east and down
at the earth where he stood. He spoke a single word, *Nun-da-ut-
sun'y,* which means the Trail Where They Cried. The old man
vanished, but my character understood what he meant. He must
walk the Trail from west to east to bring home the spirits of those
who died.

That night, after examining the relics I took from the grave
that afternoon, I went to bed. I had not even closed my eyes when
the shaman grandfather appeared at the foot of my bed as a pale
blue light. The vision both scared me and fascinated me almost
beyond belief. I tried to rationalize it to keep from being over-
powered by it. *An extension of myself, that's all.* But I couldn't
shake the vision and what I thought its presence meant: It wasn't
a character on paper who must undergo a trial. *It was me and me
alone* who must inevitably walk the Trail of Tears, in more ways
than one.

I told no one and denied the vision to myself for two years.
When I was living in Hollywood in 1987 I could run no further. I
lived in Valentino Place overlooking Paramount Studios. Rudolph
Valentino lived here when he was a star. The building had a
tunnel under the street to Paramount so he could escape his
hounding fans as he went to work. I had had a movie optioned
and received a playwriting grant, but I couldn't get work as a
scriptwriter, and L.A.—or my thoughts about it—was sickening

in a way I didn't understand. I was pushing my script about and kept getting the brush-off because, I was told, anything that was spiritual didn't make money in Hollywood. Then, one day atop the apartment building as I looked down into Paramount and over smoggy L.A., I knew the time had come to declare my values or possibly get lost in a game I was starting to play and hated. Just what it was doing to my soul and self-image anybody with his eyes half-opened could see. Anyway, I packed up and moved back home, back to the mountains of the old Cherokee Nation. That it took two years before I found the nerve to begin the walk only says, rather sadly, that I was more a prisoner than I realized. Perhaps the mountains were simply feeding and healing me after living in Hollywood. Even today, if I think too much about it, I find myself spitting forth smog, concrete, car horns, and phony voices.

# CHAPTER THIRTY-TWO

I AWAKEN TO a rooster crowing in the distance, and for a moment think that it's Sweet Talker. The sun is starting to rise and fog floats all around my tent from thick green grass. Sweat drips down my chest, but otherwise it seems normal. No sign of where *they* entered last night. Whatever happened and whatever they were doesn't frighten me this morning. Rather, I'm all the more intrigued with life. What new experiences are just now incubating and will come to me, if I will only let them? This old bit about man using only five or ten percent of his brain is surely true. How much of a man's soul does he use?

If last night's encounter was with another realm, then what I experience this afternoon is too damn close to the world we all recognize: I'm marching down the side of the road, facing the traffic as usual, when a carload of teenagers swerve toward me, to send me flying into a ditch. That I could've been killed turns me into a madman who jumps into the center of the road to throw the little bastards the finger while shouting the same at the top of my lungs.

But I can barely savor the aftermath of releasing so much rage till I begin to wonder if they won't return to appease their adolescent egos, for like it or not I recall too well what it was like when I was their age. I ran with two other kids, and one named Carl loved blood as much as he loved to pick fights. He came back from Vietnam with photographs of men he had killed there. He later turned a jeep over on top of himself and died. The other sidekick, Glenn, was my cousin. His job, it seemed, was to avoid all fights, but see how many he could talk Carl into. Glenn had more energy than he knew what to do with and was electrocuted to death when he accidentally grabbed a live wire on a construction job.

So, recalling just how passive my teenage friends were, inspires me to find a big stick just in case the gang of five or six in the killer car decide to come back to question my finger, which refused to stay in the ditch like a good dead dog. The stick is an oak limb about five feet long and as big around as a hammer handle. I'm gearing up to knock out some teeth and bang a few heads, when my anger begins to fade and I realize how haunted I would be to hurt anyone seriously, and especially a kid. If, however, it comes down to them or me, I vote for me to come out on top. I swing the stick a couple of times to get the feel of it, hoping that I'll only be amused at it all if they don't return. Which, thank goodness, they don't.

The oak limb, a perfect walking stick, makes too good a friend to throw away, and we march on as if destined to become a team. It feels right, somehow, in my hand. Just as barbells and dumbbells connect me to the solid and never-changing in life, the staff connects me more closely with the trees and the earth from which it came. Also, it is a further declaration about the odyssey I'm on. It's not everybody who walks into a café with a long stick. It, more than the feathered hat and pack, seems to dare people to investigate or to challenge. Take the waitress in Princeton, Kentucky:

I'm not sure we've got anything on the menu for your partner, she says. Want me to bring him a couple of toothpicks?

I don't mind that people, unaware of what I'm doing, poke fun at me here and there. It gives me a boost to see them come alive from their routines, and nine times out of ten, it ends up that some part of them wants to take off with me.

Resting in the shade of a tree, I sit on the ground and use my knife to skin the bark from the staff. I leave three tiny knots for personality and carve a small Third Eye in the top. I don't assume that the stick will be able to see, but it makes me feel that I know it better, just like a man becomes more confident and closer to the woman who lets him touch her in the dark. If it sounds odd for me to compare the staff to a woman, it's just that everything right now is so sensual on the journey that I can't keep from dreaming of her. Life is full of romance, passion, and poetry. When a man doesn't believe that with all his heart, he's simply out of touch with his own personal odyssey, in whatever shape or form it takes.

In Hopkinsville, Kentucky, I stop at the grave of Chief White Path, who died on the Trail in 1838. He had been appointed to a council by the Principal Chief John Ross to go to Washington to seek a treaty that would keep his people in the

South. He's buried in someone's backyard, bordering on a Trail of Tears Park which is being built by the U.S. Army. The grave stretches under a tree and I wonder how it would've affected a child to grow up in the house overlooking it. I ease my fingers against the grass-covered grave and picture the bones only a few feet from my touch. I wish I had the power to absorb instantly all that a man knew and felt in a lifetime. But come to think of it, that might not be such a smart wish. It's all I can do to deal with my own feelings, building by the day as more and more people pour me full of their stories.

Sometimes one of those stories marks me for life in only a matter of minutes, as happens with Ralph Cogin, seventy-three, just north of Nashville. He's placing letters in his mailbox as I come down a long hill with my staff bracing my steps. Even from this distance of almost one hundred yards I see that he is Cherokee. He eyes me and walks toward his house, only to stop and turn in the direction opposite me. At first, I don't grasp what he's up to. It's common for people to stop and talk after seeing me on TV or in the papers, but they do so with a child's excitement. Finally, it dawns upon me that Ralph is waiting to make sure this vagabond doesn't take his mail. When I get within twenty yards of him I begin talking about the weather and let him know what I'm doing. He relaxes and we chew the fat as I join him in his yard. He takes a lot of pride in pointing to the big yellow poplar a few hundred yards away, because that's where Grandpa Jones from *Hee Haw* lives and the house was built from Ralph's grandfather's old log barn. But it's what happens next that I'll remember for the rest of my life.

You have any children? I say.

*Had,* he says. Had a daughter. She was an actress, living in New York. She sang a song to her husband one night and went to bed. Three hours later, he came to bed and put his arms around her. She was dead. Dead at forty-two. Doctor said it was a heart attack.

I see no desire for pity as Ralph and I stare into each other's eyes. Rather, he seems simply still bewildered that his only child is gone. For my burial ritual, he breaks a small forked limb from the white pine in his yard. When I pack the gift and start to leave, he puts his arm around me.

Thank you, he says, for coming to see me.

I'm convinced that he truly believes that I came down that hill for the sole purpose of visiting him. I guess I did, at that.

I'm glad I found you at home, I say.


I'd like to claim that I enter Nashville like a man on top of the world, but I can't. This is the closest thing to a real city I've been in on the journey, and it scares me, not because I think someone will attack me but because it's a world that has grown foreign to me. Junkyards line the road; broken glass is scattered on the sidewalks. Adult book stores and peep shows promise fun inside, and a woman at the corner has red lipstick smeared on her chin.

You got a big load, she says, her speech slurred. Where you from?

The Trail of Tears, I say.

I know the feeling, honey, she says. Want to have a drink?

No, thanks, I say.

Buy *me* one? She calls out as I walk on.


It's been misting all day and dark clouds hang over downtown Nashville as I cross the bridge over the Tennessee River. Down below, a log a foot thick and twenty feet long bobs up and down in the muddy current as if it's just been spit from the giant jaws of Uktena, down there on the river's bottom. A shack sits on the bank where I imagine the homeless live. It's a direct contrast to the skyscrapers on the other side of the bridge. I ask a man in a suit for directions, and eyeing my pack, staff, and feathered hat, he becomes alarmed but is still kind enough to answer before hurrying away as fast as he can without actually breaking into a run. Already, I miss the blue jays and crows.

Trevecca Nazarene College, one mile south of downtown, gives me a cozy room in the guest house. From my second-story window, I spy on the college girls laughing as they hurry to classes. Doesn't one of them realize how much I need her? Can't she feel my gaze on the back of her neck, her lips, and curve of her hips? A list of rules is posted on my door. NO DRINKING IS ALLOWED, but my body aches as much as my heart and I'd love to open a bottle of wine with—there's got to be a heretic here on campus who believes that God celebrates flesh as much as spirit and wants to become part of an odyssey before I explode and send the window blasting across campus.

# CHAPTER THIRTY-THREE

I LEAVE MY Trail of Tears costume in the room and head for downtown. It's getting colder and the wind drives me into a busy liquor store, where a TV shows the aftermath of San Francisco's earthquake. Iron bars stick from mounds of concrete as firemen shoot giant streams of water onto burning buildings. Bodies on stretchers disappear into ambulances. The earth will not be outguessed.

I buy a half pint of brandy and hit the street. Am I hearing myself correctly? I'm now on a *street*? Pretending that I can soothe my own quake, I take a sip of the brandy and return it to my inner coat pocket.

Growing up in a small Alabama town, I hated country music and always listened to rock, blues, or folk music, which I still prefer. But I'm too old now to deny my roots and sometimes the raw honesty of a country song lets me drop the last few pounds of armor. I follow my nose to a bar called Tootsie's, where a good old boy sits with a guitar to play for tips. If he's not giving blood as he sings, he sure as hell has me fooled. Thank God, I'm not alone in Nashville on a cold wet day.

Tootsie's, I soon learn, is a famous hole in the wall. The original Grand Ole Opry began in the building just out the back door there, and this is where Hank Williams, Johnny Cash, and Merle Haggard, to name just a few, came after a show to drink, raise a little hell, and try out new songs on their peers.

This is where Willie Nelson sold his first song, says Buddy Shupe, part-owner of Tootsie's. It was called "Hello, Walls."

Buddy and I now sit in the back room of the bar, where we can talk without competing with the moans and cries of the guitar picker determined to break a few hearts and catch a dollar bill here and there to scrape through another day till his big break comes. Buddy, sixty-three, isn't much bigger than Sweet Talker, and he wears glasses so thick that his eyes appear ready to leap from his head at any second. He started smoking when he was three years old and has been on his own since he was thirteen. A coal miner in Virginia for over twenty years, he has written over one thousand songs.

I only had one recorded, he says. "California Cowboy." It was a tribute to Ronald Reagan. Guess it would help if I could write music instead of just words. I mean, I got a tune in my head for each song, but I could only whistle it to you.

Buddy's partner, Bob Moore, was once a prizefighter and stands over six feet tall. A gut pushes against a big silver belt buckle.

We're the same age, says Buddy, but I take care of him. Treat him like my little boy. You might've noticed his speech is off a little? He's a good man, but doesn't know how to tell people things.

Buddy is lighting yet another cigarette when Bob marches back to the table. He looks down at Buddy and then at me as if something's eating on him.

We've been having trouble with the law, he says. I need to check your ID and stuff before ya'll do any more talking.

I offer my driver's license and he studies it till Buddy assures him that I'm okay. He returns the ID and disappears back into the bar, where the singer continues to spill his guts on the guitar.

What kind of trouble you been having with the law? I say.

Yesterday policemen came in every ten minutes to check our customers, says Buddy. They even took some of 'em outside and made 'em walk a line. Maybe some of the bars here *should* be closed. They sell liquor to street people who are already drunk. But we don't do that here at Tootsie's. We're a landmark. The police even told the liquor store down the street not to sell to anybody who didn't have on a suit. Now, that's not right. I don't wear a suit, but I'm an American citizen and I have as much right as the next man to buy a bottle. I love America, but some people got funny ideas about how we should treat each other. Take that Klansman down in Georgia a few days ago. Said he was glad about AIDS. He hoped it would kill all the *queers*. Now, you tell me what's a *queer* anyway? Somebody who's different? Well, in some way or another we're all queer. We're all a little different. Got a call from my niece yesterday and she wanted to know if I thought the earthquake hit San Francisco because of all the homosexuals who live there. I had to explain to her about the San Adre—well, however you pronounce it—fault. We're sitting on a fault right here in Nashville and we could be next. No, this thing about sex, God gave us that luxury. Now, I'm not a religious man, but I thank God every day for what he gave me. Life is precious.

My daddy died when I was thirteen. A few days before he went, he called me and my brother to him. He put his arms around us and said whatever we did, be sure to never kill a man. I didn't know till years later that Daddy had spent time in prison because he beat a man to death with a sassafras stick over twenty-three cents in a card game.

Night falls on Nashville and snow is predicted for tomorrow as I walk the streets in cold, blowing wind. Two winos, seated in a doorway in an alley, hit on me for some change. I've been warmed not only by the brandy but by Buddy's friendliness and give the men a dollar. Or more to the bone, maybe I'm just paying for some company. One goes to get a bottle of wine and I sit with the other one, who can't look me in the eye. He hasn't shaved in four or five days and a scab covers his right cheek where he hit the sidewalk last week.

I wasn't drunk, either, he says. I slipped on a wet paper bag. Smoke?

He pours tobacco into a paper, rolls it, licks it, and lights it with a cigarette lighter similar to the one Ray used back in Golconda. He says he came to Nashville to make it as a singer, but got discouraged and gave up.

I don't care anymore, he says. I live from day to day and that's all I ask for. That may sound bitter, but I'm not. Can't everybody thread the golden needle. Those that make it, more power to them.

Do you have a family? I ask.

Some cousins left, he says. But they're back in North Carolina. They don't know how to reach me and I never bother with them. It's just as well. We never were very close. Well, we were when we were young, but people drift apart. Bet you've made a lot of friends on this walk?

I'm not sure that they're friends, I say. But I've met a lot of people I'm gonna miss.

Yeah, he says, licking the cigarette again. People come and go. But friends are hard to find. I wish I had something to give you. I got a little Cherokee blood from my mother's side.

He digs into his pockets and finds a button. He lowers his head in shame.

Nothing, he says.

How about the button? I say.

But it ain't nothing, he says. Just an old button that came off my shirt.

His friend returns with a bottle of wine and I leave them smacking their lips. When I turn the corner, I fish into my pocket for the button. I can't say exactly why, but it means as much to me as the rose blossom I received from Lewis Day back in Arkansas. Maybe it's special because of the look in the wino's eyes when I said it would be buried with the other gifts—just like it was a piece of gold. Maybe I've simply had too much brandy and am caught up in all this down-and-out country music I soaked up in Tootsie's. In any event, I'm sad tonight. I'm just another country singer on the streets of Nashville. My heart is full, but I don't have a guitar and I couldn't carry a tune in a bucket if my life depended on it. If I were truly strong and courageous, perhaps I would chant at the top of my lungs to move people on the street with what the birds, animals, trees, rivers, and stars have given me along the Trail. It's not easy to accept that I'm just a man on the street in the night with liquor on his breath. What happened to my clothing of blue sky? Where are the spirits who floated into my chest to fill me with magic and connect me with time eternal?

# CHAPTER THIRTY-FOUR

I AWAKE THE next morning with a hangover and his faithful companion, humiliation. I have betrayed any nobility granted me on the Trail. The staff leans against the wall and its Third Eye burns into me. I cannot outrun the truth. Last night leveled me to the ground. An arrogance that was trying to root in my soul from all the newspaper and TV coverage had the breath knocked out of it. That's okay. I needed it. I'm no better than the wino who gave me the button. For that matter, no one is. We're all just passing through, and to forget that is to show our asses. I don't really expect you to probe your soul as you sit there in your easy chair. You're probably not hung over anyway. Just bear with me for a minute longer and I'll stop preaching to myself.

First, let me make a confession. There's a gap between the time I left the winos and I got back to this room. Curious as to how I tried to fill the void? I went to a pay phone and called Venda. Her voice was as warm and inviting as her lips had been that day on the blanket by the giant turquoise spring. I didn't realize just how much I had fallen for her till we talked. She was a column of light coming down from the rainy night. To passers-by I may have appeared like a man with a giant chest and big strong arms. But hanging on to the phone, I was really no bigger than the hummingbird I found with its beak stuck in the phone case in Mansfield, where Venda lives. I was, however, alive, and my wings were beating a mile a minute as I told her how much I missed her and wanted to hold her. *Now* it becomes clear what is really on my back this morning: I lost control last night. I got down on my knees and reached for someone to love.

My body feels like hell as I get out of bed and take a shower as if to wash away the poison I put in it last night. When I dry myself, I stand naked before the mirror to study this flesh that surrounds me. It isn't ego or vanity that draws me here. It's almost thirty years of discipline from lifting weights and eating right to build this temple that helps me believe in myself and reactivate this morning's darkened spirit. It's okay, I tell myself, to have crashed against the cliff last night and be shipwrecked and saved by a woman on the other end of a phone. So it is with an odyssey. A man must sometimes ride the waves of his emotions.

When I leave Nashville, the still-darkened sky is spitting snow. As if yet trying to redeem myself from the drunken ship-wreck last night, I walk the most miles I've covered in a single day; thirty-three miles down the Trail takes me into Murfrees-boro. What a Great Medicine to become so exhausted that the body, mind, and spirit reunite in the kingdom of sleep.

*  *  *

I not only awake feeling whole the next morning, but the sky is once again its famous blue. As I approach Woodbury, the mountains begin to appear for the first time on the journey. They are towering gates to the Deep South, to that most blessed place to a wanderer, to a place called *home*. To see my father again, who I believed had died in my dream in the Ozarks, will be a joyous sight, but to see my mother and put my arms around her will reconfirm the mercy and tenderness of God. I have only to see her face to find reason to live. For those who are not close to their parents, I understand how my journey is little or nothing at all, because they walk the Trail of Tears every day of their lives. They have been moved from their homes and driven to a land no map can show. It is from my father's stubbornness and determination that I draw the strength to put one foot in front of the other each day. It is from my mother's sensitivity that I gain the power to see the poetry in those I meet. Yes, dear mountains, you're a sight for sore eyes. I have been longing for you almost as much as faith in love itself.

It's dark when I reach Woodbury and get a fish sandwich in Hardee's. I was stopped on the road early this morning by Phil Jones. He had seen me on Nashville TV a couple of days ago and invited me to stay with him and his daughters tonight. We are to meet here, but there's no sign of him and he has no phone. In a way, I hope he doesn't show up, for I'm tired and he had mentioned going to a friend's house for dinner. All I want to do is rest and dream of home.

Still, there was something in Phil, tall and slender and my age, that made me more curious than most folks. Now that I see him arriving in the parking lot with his two daughters, Ellen, eight, and Ronda, nine, I'm reminded just what it is that intrigues me about him. He seems to have undergone something that might reduce others to ashes. A carpenter, he recently divorced a musician in the Nashville Symphony. His daughters live with her except on the weekends. This breakup could certainly scar a man in a discreet way, but by the end of the night, I discover a secret that I wouldn't have guessed.

I hope you didn't eat, says Phil as I come from Hardee's with my pack and staff. My friend I told you about has fixed dinner for us.

I'm starved, I say.

He introduces me to his daughters and I melt. They're not only beautiful, but radiate impish grins; magic plays up their sleeves.

How'd the soccer game go? I ask as we hit a country road.

We lost, says Ellen, but we had fun anyway.

I'm always a bit nervous about meeting strangers in their home. If I don't like them I feel trapped for an evening, and trying to carry on worthy conversation in such a situation around a dinner table is like eating broken glass.

We take a dirt road now and pass a roaring bonfire with flames six feet high. A party is in full swing and some of the Tennessee rabble-rousers loom out of the dark on a wagon loaded with hay. I wish we were stopping here. Their laughter makes the hills and stars a carnival, flickering before the enormous fire.

But like an answered prayer, we move on down the road to discover a second fire where Phil's friend, Leo Collins, lives. He's our age, with shoulder-length hair, and is a jack-of-all-trades. He moved here several years ago from New York and says he could never go back. His friend, Rex, visiting from Miami, has also decided to move here.

I called my wife tonight, he says, and told her to start pack-

ing. I got two children and there's so much drug dealing going
down on the street I'm afraid to let 'em even play in the front
yard. I like it here in the hills. At least it's sane.

Some people, says Leo, think people in Tennessee are just
barefooted hicks.

Yes, says Phil, but we're that and more.

The bonfire, popping and crackling, blazes fifty yards from a
century-old log house and Leo has wrapped pork, potatoes, and
carrots in foil to place them in the coals to cook while we sit on
boards stretched between logs. The hills surround us and there's
not an electric light in sight. Except for the night I spent on the
hill at Zion's Order, I don't recall the stars being so bright anywhere along the Trail. But like anything as magical as the heavens, we see it through our emotions. I'm happy to be once again
with strangers who make me feel welcome. Ellen and Ronda have
joined Leo's two kids in the dark to play hide and seek, and their
shouts and laughter blend with the fire's dancing shadows to turn
the night into a timeless world free of grinding brakes and gun-
shots.

I'm so tired that I can do little more than stare into the fire.
It and it alone seems to understand what I have experienced on
the Trail, and when Rex asks me to tell him about the trip, I can
only look into his eyes and hope that he can see that he asks the
impossible. I want to be wise and answer with stories that will
leave him and the others entranced, but I can't tonight. Tonight I
am too close to too much I have thought and felt along the way
and my body rules my mind. I am a dumb man, content just to sit
with others around a fire. Please, this is all I ask. Just let me *be*
with you. Let me enjoy your voices and faces in the flickering
light. Forgive me that I have so little to give. I'll make it up to you
the next time around.

But as tired as I am I can still see a little, and I get a clue to what has happened to Phil that seems to have scarred him for life when I discover that Leo was one of the first Marines in Vietnam.

Were you there too? I ask.

No, says Phil.

He and Leo exchange glances with a meaning that's over my head. Maybe I'm even more tired than I realize, for I was certain I sensed something about the war in Vietnam in Phil's eyes, as if he lost something or someone there. When we get to his house, Ellen and Ronda go to bed to watch *Saturday Night Live*.

Aren't you coming to bed with us, Daddy? says Ronda.

In a few minutes, he says. Get the bed warm.

Okay, Daddy, she says, closing the bedroom door.

It's below freezing tonight and wind blows through cracks in Phil's simple little house, where flint arrowheads and scrapers lay about on shelves and tables as if trying to marry the past to the present. He lights a kerosene heater at the foot of a mattress on the floor where I'll sleep tonight.

I like your friend, Leo, I say.

He's a good guy, he says.

I guess the war was pretty hard on him? I say.

The war was hard on a lot of people, he says. Did you go?

I was lucky, I say. I got a high lottery number in the draft. What kept you out?

Myself, he says, a hint of sadness in his voice.

I don't get it, I say.

I went to Canada, he says. Spent nine years there. Landed in Toronto and moved on to Newfoundland. That's where I learned to be a carpenter.

Did your family come to see you? I say.

My father came once, he said.

Phil is the first draft dodger I ever knowingly met. That he and Leo, who I gather may have killed several men in Vietnam, can be friends after following such different paths is certainly a salute to humanity. But let's not bullshit here. This sends my feeble mind to spinning: They must've gone crazy missing this great place called *home*. Yes, I have home, home, home on the brain tonight. I'm so close I can taste it, and not totally unlike the Cherokee who were driven from their home by the U.S. Army, Phil was exiled from his home, his whole country, because he chose not to go to Vietnam and destroy someone else's home. Leo, on the other hand, went to Vietnam to protect his home in America. Who is the real hero?

I truly wish I had a hero. I wish I believed in a great leader. It's a sobering day when a man admits he has neither. That's one of the reasons I undertook this humble odyssey. I hoped to find at least a shadow of a hero in myself. I can't swear that I have, but I feel I'm on the right trail. From time to time, I find one of his tracks.

Phil goes into the bedroom and I crawl into my sleeping bag on the mattress. The red-orange glow of the kerosene heater is a tiny sun rising on the horizon of my feet as I fall asleep with Ronda and Ellen laughing in their father's arms; *Saturday Night Live* mixes with the warring wind, sneaking through cracks in the walls and into my dreams.

# CHAPTER THIRTY-FIVE

M Y LOWER BACK, leg, and left ankle are giving me hell, but I'm only a week from home and the thought drives me, fills me with the passion of a man possessed. My third leg, my staff, helps me up Cumberland Mountain and across it in a single day and part of the night into Dunlap in the Sequatchie Valley. It's here, on a deserted road, that I enter a small grocery to overhear a woman in tight faded jeans tell the cashier she knifed her husband.

You knifed your own husband? I say.

It didn't hurt him much, she said. It was the gunshot that killed him.

He must've been pretty mean to you, I say.

No, she says. But he pissed me off. Caught him with another woman, she laughs, and the jury let me off scot-free.

It's no amusement park to walk in the dark after leaving a

killer with a loud laugh. She seemed so proud of what she had
done that I expected her at any second to pull out a medal she
had made for herself. Then, too, the Trail is spooky tonight because Halloween is only a few days away and ghosts, made of
sheets, hang from limbs in front of a few farmhouses. They dance
in the wind while jack-o'-lanterns smile up from the depths of a
fiery hell. It's more than a rumor that folks back in these isolated
mountains have been known to shoot first and dare anyone to ask
questions later.

But when I arrive on the east side of Signal Mountain, overlooking Chattanooga, I'm so thrilled that I actually shout into the
night like a warrior—or a fool—because I *know* this town, built at
the base of Lookout Mountain, which stretches to the south to
face my home. Down there in the valley, its million lights twin-
kling in the night make me feel that I am part of the stars. It
doesn't matter that I'm only a man who owns little more than is
on his back. I celebrate the great and wonderful illusion that
tonight I am immortal. Nothing can stop me now. I am as strong
as the rock cliff to my left, small waterfalls shooting to the earth
in moonlight. Here, at last, I am back in the old Cherokee Nation.

The next day I walk into Chattanooga and step onto the
bridge that crosses the Tennessee River. When I'm halfway to the
other side, I remove my pack. I lean against the iron railing and
look down into the water, home of Long Man, the river god, as
well as Uktena. Near the bank, over one hundred yards away, a
great white crane stands in water up to his delicate knees. He
faces me as if he knows why I'm here. He is as still as Lookout
Mountain only two miles south of us.

Some fifty yards to the left of the crane is Ross's Landing.
This is where Chief John Ross and his family boarded a boat

headed for Indian Territory. They sailed down the wide and rolling Tennessee River past great farms where horses and cattle
livened pastures and hillsides. White men and their slaves waved
from the banks as they burned brush, smoke streaking the blue
sky. Fishermen gawked and pointed at the departing Indians.

When Chief Ross and his wife completed the boat trip, they
had a horse-drawn carriage to carry them westward. Everything
was going smoothly till a heavy snow slowed them and Ross's
wife caught a cold after giving her blanket to a sick child. The
next day she could not stand and she soon died. Her only coffin
was the earth itself. Like the poorest Cherokee, she was buried by
the side of the road.

I put on my pack and walk on across the bridge. When I
reach the other side, the crane lifts from the water as if Long Man
blows his great wings to give a helping hand. The graceful bird
takes my breath as it vanishes across the river into a grove of oaks
and willows.

Except for a few home-cooked meals on the Trail—Phil
made corn bread and scrambled eggs for breakfast—I've been
eating from grocery stores and cafés. It's a real luxury, and a bit
bizarre, to enter a chic little restaurant in downtown Chattanooga
for lunch. I'm so high from being this close to home that I'm only
amused when the business people—dressed like magazine and
TV clones—gawk at my oak stick and the rest as if I just crawled
out of the woods. I don't begrudge their money-grabbing lives.
I'm aware that underneath it all rivers of emotions and buried
dreams twist and turn, seeking their own unique identities. Or
am I, as is often the case by standard practices, being too romantic? Maybe these people don't have a trace of courage and imagination to become anything more than what advertisers and peers
pour into their brains. Whatever, I welcome them into my odyssey as I eat lasagna and sip a glass of red wine. (Yeah, I forgave

myself for getting loaded in Nashville. I don't usually get that stupid.) I do, however, now write a letter to Venda with an apology about the phone call that night. I'm not ashamed of having broken down and called like a man on a raft at sea, but I fear I may have gotten too graphic about all I wanted to do with her. Little, if nothing more, can really come of having met her. I have no desire to marry anyone. I need a woman who is as tender and loving as her, but who also is as free as me. I'm not complaining. I take love in whatever shape or form and for however long fate or passion blesses me. Of course, it's much easier now that I'm back in the mountains to feel strong and not so lonely. A man can't make love to the mountains, but he can be fed and comforted by them. I could live without them, as the exiled Cherokee did and do, but I would not have a certain power they give a man who grows up in them. It is, of course, a dangerous power, for it makes a man forever want to climb higher, while in the same breath forcing him to realize that he is so small. I sometimes pray to the mountains for their wisdom. They speak so softly and so slowly, I sometimes think I must listen for their answer till the day I die. If it sounds as though I place the mountains alongside God, it's true. I cannot make the distinction. If I could, I think I would become frightened. Is it really possible that in one hundred and forty miles I'll be *home*?

If I turned due south here in Chattanooga, I could cut almost one hundred miles from the walk, because Fort Payne, Alabama, is only fifty miles away. But it's important to me that I first walk to New Echota, Georgia, to touch the earth of the Cherokee Capital at the time of the removal in 1838. From there I will walk westward, over Lookout Mountain, and down into the valley of my cabin, high on a hill.

Only a few miles south of Chattanooga I leave Tennessee to cross over into Georgia. That afternoon I arrive in Tunnel Hill, where my favorite cousin, Eddy, lives. He isn't in from work yet, but he met me on the Trail this morning and gave me the key to his house. I go inside and barely have my pack off when I discover the house is surrounded by four policemen and a German shepherd police dog ready to tear my leg off. Okay, throw your stick out first and come out with your hands . . .

I sure am sorry, says the officer. We got a call saying some homeless-looking guy broke in with a pack, to steal stuff.

My cousin *does* have a good sense of humor, I say. But I'm not sure it's *that* good.

No, no, says the officer. Some woman, a neighbor, phoned.

My cousin, Eddy, arrives and we go to Dalton for Chinese food. I have a child's excitement about seeing him, but something isn't right. I wonder if this great high I'm on which so connects me to the birds and trees and some timeless realm is separating us. I want to lift people with this feeling. I want to radiate the magic of all the wonderful folks I've met along the Trail. Life is good. Life, in fact, is just damn fantastic. Man must slow down to *see* that. But I fear I may be sounding like a fanatic who has just wandered from the wilderness with a beard dragging the ground. But, no, I haven't gone over the edge. I'm careful not to say too much. We're simply in different places.

We return to his house and he shows me his new computer. At first, I'm amazed at all the great lines and curves it offers with the press of a button. Anything that helps man create and progress gets my nod, but it soon becomes repetitious. I become sad because we are not looking at each other. Our eyes have become prisoners of the screen, the Great Eye. It, like the TV screen, has replaced the fire in the cave. Men are no longer gathering in the cold night to stay warm and release their spirits through stories.

We no longer look into each other's souls. Maybe we're afraid of what we might see.

I go to bed with the feeling I have failed to connect with someone I love. But, of course, it is *only* a feeling, my uncontrolled craving to be home with my family and back in my spot on the hill.

New Echota, Georgia, was the capital of the Cherokee Nation in 1838 when the U.S. army herded the Indians into thirteen prison camps. I now walk through a fog lifting from the historic site of the courthouse, which was burned to the ground by the fire-happy soldiers. This is also where the *Cherokee Phoenix* was published in both English and Cherokee, consisting of eighty-five characters.

The Cherokee are the only American Indians to have their own alphabet. Sequoyah (George Gist), who invented the alphabet, didn't tickle his wife to death with the idea. Lame in one leg, he worked on his dream for years in a shack behind his house. His wife began to think he was a bum. After all, a grown man wasn't supposed to spend hours day after day making strange marks on paper, was he? She had some friends try to talk a little sense into his hard head. When he failed to listen, she went to his shack and burned all his work to ashes.

Sequoyah started again from scratch. When he finally got his dream ironed out, he called friends and neighbors into his home. He sent his daughter deep into the woods and had someone speak a word—any word he liked—and then made marks on a piece of paper. The daughter was called from the woods and he presented her with the paper. She spoke the word and the onlookers ran from the house because they feared Sequoyah was using witchcraft. In the following months he began to teach the Cherokee how to read and write.

It's Sunday morning here at New Echota and sunlight comes through the tall pines to shine into the fog and onto hundreds of spiderwebs in the grass. It's easy to see how the town was laid out, for new buildings now imitate the old ones.

As the fog lifts I walk on down the old dirt street of New Echota, to the hand-dug well that remains behind the site of the house where Elias Boudinot lived. He was editor of the *Cherokee Phoenix* and joined forces with his brother, Stand Watie, Major Ridge and his son, John, and others to sign the Treaty of New Echota, which helped lead to the removal in 1838. Like the Ridges, Boudinot was later killed as a traitor in Tahlequah. A knife got his back. A tomahawk split open his head.

The little museum here won't open until this afternoon, but I phoned yesterday and spoke to Frankie, the site's manager. He wouldn't let me camp in the field here where the town once stood, but he agreed to meet me here and show me around. It's not him, of course, that I came to see. I simply—*simply?*—want to connect the old capital here at New Echota to the current one in Tahlequah with my feet and heart. My whole body chills as I face once again the fact that an entire nation—or those who survived —was moved to another part of the country like wild horses to the dog food company.

Frankie shows up in his truck and takes me into the museum. He lets me pick a piece of broken china from a box filled with hundreds of such pieces found on the site. But it's the mockingbird we see when we go back outside that has a story worth telling.

There that bird is *again,* says Frankie.

The mockingbird sits on a limb above his truck. It darts down to the window and back to the tree again.

What'd you mean? I say, having said nothing about my stay with Dr. Noble in the Bird Clan or how all the birds have been my friends along the Trail.

Just look at him, says Frankie. See how he flies down to my window? He wants inside, and I can't figure out why. He first showed up two months ago and tried to get into the museum. Sure beats me.

Maybe he's trying to tell you something, I say.

I'm tempted to roll down my window, says Frankie, and let him get inside. I could take him far enough away that he couldn't find his way back here.

I don't say a word, but the correlation between what Frankie wants to do with the mockingbird and what happened to the Cherokee jolts me with an eerie uneasiness. He wants to trap the bird and take it away because, of course, it spots his truck, certainly a breathtaking piece of art. But he doesn't mention anything about the mockingbird's beautiful talent. I guess his philosophy is simply Metal Before Songs. *Things* Before Nature. Anyway, I shake his hand, thank him for the chip of Cherokee china in my pocket, and head—finally—for Alabama.

I'm only a few miles down the road when a truck passes and the passenger says hello by spotting my chest with a mouthful of spit. Yes, sir, down here in Dixie we sure like to make folks feel at home. I got to hand it to the old boy, though, not many of us rednecks can spit-hit a target from a moving truck. I do wish, however, he had had the dignity to have stopped and challenged me to a Spit Duel in this sagebrush field to my right. Like all Southerners, I was taught as a child to spit, and hate to brag, but

I'm pretty damn good. Yes, sir, I think I could've spit his eyeball clean out of his dumb-shit head. Oh, I wish I were in the land of cotton . . .

Yes, I'm getting giddy. I've walked almost nine hundred miles in sixty days and home is only twenty-four hours away. When, every few hours, it soaks in just how warm and kind most of the people have been along the Trail and that I'm safe and still in one piece and won't have to walk anymore, I begin to laugh in a way I didn't know I was capable of. It is the short private laugh of a man who has surrendered, at last, to fate and gained a new hold on faith. In other words, I'm enjoying this rare and awesome flight of discreet immortality with veins of hysteria. I'm actually amused that the poor idiot spit on me. He's *down there,* while I'm *up here.* Let it last, oh, please, let it last.

# CHAPTER THIRTY-SIX

LOOKOUT MOUNTAIN FINALLY looms into view and I welcome it like a lost lover. It's red and yellow with autumn leaves, while patches of great gray cliffs line the top. A crow calls from somewhere among the trees and a hawk circles in the distance. Cattle and horses graze to my left. Orange pumpkins dot the field to my right.

I'm near the mountain's base when I spot a road to my left leading to my great-grandmother, buried near the home of the last Indian Agent in Georgia. That I, too, will become bones is no problem. Just let me make it over the mountain. Let me see my mother and father and home once more.

I like the pain of climbing Lookout Mountain. It is the pain of love as much as the suffering of the flesh.

It's late afternoon when I see the ALABAMA WELCOMES YOU sign. It's twenty more miles to home and I'm only a hundred yards back in my home state when a big black dog runs from the woods toward me. I lift my staff ready for the attack, but the dog, a Labrador retriever, looks at me with almost human eyes as if he knows me. He marches in front of me as though to lead the way. I've seen hundreds of dogs along the Trail and a few followed me for a minute or two, only to return home and become flickers of memory. But not this dog, black as a crow. He stays with me for a half mile and I finally shout at him to *go home.* He won't listen and ignores the small rocks I throw at him. It hurts to do it, but I poke him gently with my stick. His human eyes simply stare into mine as if I must *see* that he is mine and I am his. But I don't want him. He belongs to somebody and I've come too far now to end the odyssey with a beautiful creature like him getting splattered by a car or truck. I poke him again with my staff and shout with my most rugged voice to *go home.* He slows for only a few seconds before his happy tail wags to lead the way down the Trail.

By sundown, Crow Dog and I are one helluva team. Sorry, Bunny, but wood can never win over flesh and blood. Crow Dog isn't afraid to fight either. When three dogs dart from a house barking like an attack pack, he charges them and they run the other way.

It's that fine delicate line between twilight and night when Crow Dog and I reach the dirt road that descends Lookout Mountain into the valley where I live. The lights of Fort Payne twinkle to the left, while to the right the lights of Valley Head look like stars. It's there that the last Cherokee Council Tree in the area was destroyed by lightning in 1936. Sequoyah taught his alphabet in both towns. Now, though Cherokee blood is rich among the citizens, no one in the county speaks the ancient language.

No one lives on this dirt road and the thick trees make it so dark that it's hard to see. Here, around this curve, is where my grandfather and I once climbed into the woods to hunt for ginseng. When the Cherokee searched for ginseng, they passed the first three plants. They dug the fourth one and placed a bead in the hole to thank the plant spirit. As I walk on I wonder how many such bead offerings hide all around just beneath the surface in the night.

When we reach the valley, we must walk a couple of miles along a busy road, and Crow Dog runs in front of a car. I close my eyes, knowing my ears will still hear the most horrible of sounds. But I'm wrong. He appears on the other side of the highway as if he became only air when the car roared over him. How can a man get so damn close to a dog in only a few hours? Come on, Crow Dog. We're almost there.

We pass the reservoir, silver in moonlight, where I found the artifacts when the lake was being built and the vision, or whatever it was, appeared to me that night in my bedroom. The circle is almost completed. I've come thirty-five miles since this morning, with only one more mile to go. I can't believe my dream is about to come true. I've never been so thankful in all my life. Is it possible with all my wanderings and hungers that up until now I haven't really been living?

Crow Dog stays at my side as if I am a blind man as I tap my way through the dark the last hundred yards toward home. Then something happens like I've never experienced and I hope it never happens again. I see the lights coming from my parents' house back up in the woods. As I get closer, the house itself appears, only to vanish before my very eyes. The light is still there and much stronger—like a glowing sphere—but the house is *gone*. It's too much for my tired mind to grasp. In fact, it's not something of the mind. It's of the human soul and spirit. *Home,* what I crave above all else, has vanished just when I thought I began to understand its real meaning and importance. Now I really am a blind man with a dog and a stick on the Trail. I have experienced too much and stepped into another realm, where a man is humbled to the point of total dumbness. I know nothing. Nothing except that I am a blind man exhausted in the night. It is a fear I did not know lived within me. If only I could see again. If only I could get back home.

Then—I don't know how many seconds later—the lights dim in the woods and the house reappears. Home is at my fingertips. Now, however, a white ghostly figure looms from the dark near a small light on the ground. It turns out to be my mother in a white robe. I throw my arms around her and feel no shame to be both man and boy in the same breath.

I heard your stick tapping the road, she says.

The light at her feet is a candle in a paper bag. My sister put it there when she arrived from Atlanta tonight. On it is an arrow pointing toward the house, as it says *this way home.* I kiss the earth and follow that arrow to the door. To see my mother, father, and sister alive once more is to sleep like I never slept before.

# EPILOGUE

PREPARING FOR THE sweatlodge, I begin a three-day fast and consume only water. During this time, however, I feed Crow Dog the finest food. I can't swear that he was a guide sent to me by the Spirit World, as if the woods, from where he came, created him from earth, roots, and leaves. In fact, I begin to think of whoever raised him and how he must miss him. It hurts to consider parting with him—he loves it here in the woods—but I put an announcement on the local radio and a man comes to claim him. I don't fully trust the man, for Crow Dog appeared twenty miles from where the man lives in Fort Payne.

I can't swear in blood, says the man, that he's mine. He's been gone two months and could've grown a lot. He's not a year old yet. But I'm pretty sure it's him. Figure somebody got him into his car and took off to the Georgia line, where he took up with you.

I feel like I betray my friend as I load him into the backseat of the man's car. As long as I live I'll never forget the look in his eyes as I close the door.

That night I can't stop thinking about Crow Dog. A bit down, I phone my friend, Susan, to tell her that I'll return the pack and other camping equipment after the sweatlodge ritual and I'm fully rested from the trip. I can't help but mention the loss of Crow Dog.

I come and go so much anyway, I say. It wouldn't have been fair to him.

Debbie and I would've loved to have him, says Susan. You could've seen him when you wanted to.

This only makes me feel worse. If only I had waited a few more days before putting the announcement on the radio. . . . Such is fate, or so I tell myself to try to escape the sorrow of parting with Crow Dog. He was the only one who walked with me.


On the afternoon of my third day of fasting I climb the hill to my cabin to enter the sweatlodge. I build a fire inside, where stones as big as my head encircle it. While the heat builds within the structure, I stay outside to call crows into the towering trees. Several answer, but none will light. Perhaps they spot me on the cabin porch or the smoke from the sweatlodge scares them away. But I'm not disappointed, for simply to see their black wings against the sky is enough to put me in touch with all those I saw along the Trail. In the near distance, I also hear two or three blue jays singing their wild and beautiful songs. It is, of course, the crane I seek. To see it glide over me right now would be the greatest of signs. A hawk circles in the distance and I love its grace, but no crane appears and the blue jays stop their songs. As evening comes, I'm left alone with only a breeze and smoke rising from the canvas-covered dome.

I enter the sweatlodge. The fire blazes from the pit in the center of the earth. It's hot in here now and I remove all my clothes to sit by the fire. I ease my fingers into a gourd filled with water and sprinkle it on the stones. They hiss as if alive and steam rises from them as sweat begins to come from my skin. I put a few drops of water to my lips before I begin to seek a song I believe will arise from all I experienced on the journey, which, of course, continues now as the fire pops and crackles.

To the fire I add a piece of bark from an oak at the base of this hill; it was struck by lightning. When the bark blazes, I see myself back on the Trail in the thunderstorm. I add more water to the stones and when steam rises, I begin to search for feelings through sounds rising from my gut and up through my chest and heart. My mouth opens to create a slow and mournful sound, like that of the wind howling softly through the trees so far in the distance that a listener must be dedicated to be certain it even exists at all.

As this slow, sad song continues, I see myself in flashes along the Trail. Birds, trees, and graves. Rivers and strangers, kind as songs themselves. My tent in moonlight. Smoke rising to the stars.

Darkness falls and the stars appear as I continue my song, given to me, in part, by all those I met on the Trail. It is, however, not so much a song of sadness as a song of acceptance. I am only just another man, like all men, on the Trail of Tears. To laugh at myself and treat those I meet with compassion is the best I can do till I return to the earth, which I now scoop into my hand and smear on my naked wet body, hot from the steam and flame.

From my hat I take the feathers—crow, owl, blue jay, and turkey —and brush against my flesh as the slow chant continues into the night, and I seek a vision. But it never comes. I'm left alone again with my naked body, the fire and my song, telling yet again that I am only a man. Not a myth come alive and not a hero. Only a man on a hill in the night. But as the truth seeps in, I find perhaps a greater power through it than through a vision. I am only a man, but what a fantastic creature. He seeks the supernatural while the extraordinary is all around him. I walked nine hundred miles and entered into an odyssey that will feed me for the rest of my life. My faith in both God and man has stepped to the next plane and I made it home safe and sound. I literally watched a dream come true. How much richer can I ask to become? And yet, I no sooner say this than I'm concerned that what I did to unite me with others will, in a way, separate me from them. How can anyone really know what I experienced on the Trail, if he hasn't done it himself? Dear reader, have I failed you? Have I been honest and clear enough for you to make this walk with me?

A week later I'm rested, but a fear begins to sneak my way. My clothing of blue sky is starting to fade. I'm driving my car now and everything is speeding up. I'm checking the TV listings and pressing the remote control unit much too often.

Growing restless, I load the pack and camping equipment into my car and go to return them to Susan and Debbie, who live in downtown Fort Payne. I haven't seen them since I've been back and it feels good to hug them as we say hello.

We have somebody else, says Susan, you might want to say hello to.

Yeah? I squint.

She takes me into the next room, and here is Crow Dog. He showed up at their house about a week ago, as if he knew just where he was going. He now jumps up on me and I ease my fingers into the hair on his head. Just how he chose this spot over thousands of others in town, I do not question. It is the way of the Trail. His human eyes seem to say he's ready to hit the road again.

*So am I, Crow Dog. So am I.*

# BIBLIOGRAPHY

Cromer, Marie West, *Modern Indians of Alabama.* Birmingham, Alabama, Southern University Press, 1984.

Ehle, John, *Trail of Tears.* New York, Doubleday, 1988.

Mooney, James, *Myths of the Cherokee.* Washington, Government Printing Office, 1900. (Republished, St. Clair Shores, Michigan, Scholarly Press, 1970.)

Woodward, Grace, *The Cherokees.* Norman, Oklahoma, University of Oklahoma Press, 1963.

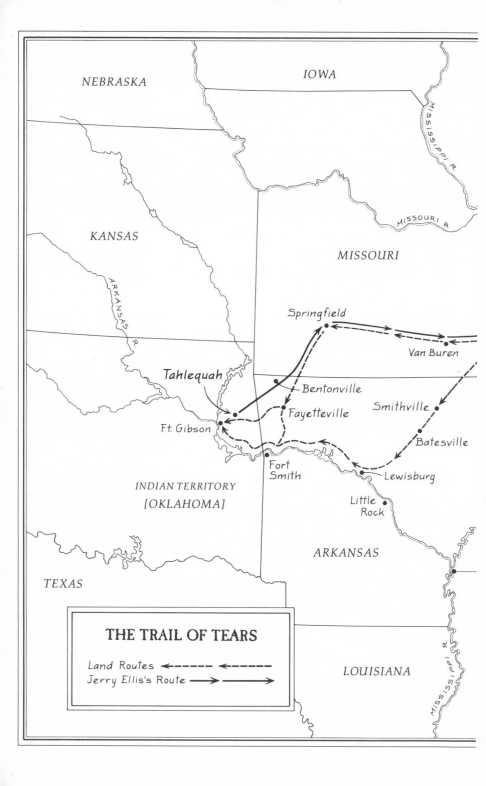

NEBRASKA

IOWA

KANSAS

MISSOURI

MISSISSIPPI R.

MISSOURI R.

ARKANSAS R.

Springfield

Van Buren

Tahlequah

Bentonville

Fayetteville

Smithville

Ft. Gibson

Batesville

Fort Smith

Lewisburg

INDIAN TERRITORY
[OKLAHOMA]

Little
Rock

ARKANSAS

TEXAS

MISSISSIPPI R.

LOUISIANA

## THE TRAIL OF TEARS

Land Routes ←------ ←------

Jerry Ellis's Route ⟶ ⟶